Nell McAndrew's
guide to
RUNNING

Nell McAndrew
& Lucy Waterlow

Everything
you need to know
to train, race
and more

B L O O M S B U R Y
LONDON · NEW YORK · SYDNEY

NOTE

While every effort has been made to ensure that the content of this book is as technically accurate and as sound as possible, neither the author nor the publishers can accept responsibility for any injury or loss sustained as a result of the use of this material.

Bloomsbury Sport
An imprint of Bloomsbury Publishing Plc

50 Bedford Square
London
WC1B 3DP
UK

1385 Broadway
New York
NY 10018
USA

www.bloomsbury.com

BLOOMSBURY and the Diana logo are trademarks of Bloomsbury Publishing Plc

First published 2015

British Library Cataloguing-in-Publication Data

A catalogue record for this book is available from the British Library.

ISBN: 978-1-4729-0575-8

ePDF: 978-1-4729-0842-1

ePub: 978-1-4729-0841-4

10 9 8 7 6 5 4 3 2 1

Acknowledgements

Cover photograph © Eddie Macdonald

Printed and bound in China by Hung Hing Printing Group Limited

Bloomsbury Publishing Plc makes every effort to ensure that the papers used in the manufacture of our books are natural, recyclable products made from wood grown in well-managed forests. Our manufacturing processes conform to the environmental regulations of the country of origin.

To find out more about our authors and books visit www.bloomsbury.com. Here you will find extracts, author interviews, details of forthcoming events and the option to sign up for our newsletters.

CONTENTS

INTRODUCTION

Welcome to my guide to running. Whether you're reading this because you want to learn how to get started or – like me – you're always looking for tips on how to get faster, I hope it helps you achieve your goals.

Running is my passion, it's more than just a hobby. As a busy mum of two, it's my stress relief and my favourite way to unwind. I've always loved the feeling exercise gives me. It makes me feel alive, energised and more confident. It also means I enjoy my food more and I don't feel guilty about having treats like chocolate!

Exercise has become a way of life for me and I couldn't live without it. Growing up in Leeds, Yorkshire, I was always sporty. At school I was on the netball team and tried karate for a while. I loved being active and trying new things but I was never particularly good at, or interested in, running at this time. Like many people, I think not being great at running whilst at school made me reluctant to try it when I was older. So instead throughout my twenties when I was working as a model, I kept fit at the gym and did workouts like those seen on my Peak Energy fitness DVDs. I would run on the treadmill or go for the odd run around the park, but it wasn't until I signed up for the London Marathon in 2004 (more on that later in the book) that I started to take running more seriously – and I haven't looked back. It turns out I was much better at it than I thought! I was 30 then and ran my marathon personal best (PB) time of 2 hours 54 minutes when I was 38. I achieved all my other PBs that year

Far left: I think I was trying to run away from my grandma here!

Left: I'm not so sure about those running shorts!

too (18 minutes 43 seconds for 5k, 29 minutes 21 seconds for 5 miles, 36 minutes 54 seconds for 10k, and 1 hour 21 minutes for the half marathon). So it just goes to show, it's never too late to start or to improve. I'm now in my forties and I still believe I can run faster. I love the challenge of pushing myself to see what I can do.

Anyone who already has the running bug will know how fun and addictive it can be, but it's not always easy to get started, or to stay motivated. So I hope by sharing my passion for the sport, and what I've learnt along the way, I can give you some support, encouragement and inspiration.

Since June 2012, I have written a monthly column for *Women's Running* magazine outlining how I combine motherhood and training. I've always wanted to write a book and I'm delighted to finally put pen to paper after joining forces with journalist Lucy Waterlow, a fellow running devotee. Lucy has interviewed me a number of times over the years and we bonded over our love of running and racing. This illustrates something else I love about the sport – no matter what your background or ability, you can always make friends through running.

I love hearing about other people's running experiences which is why I've included stories from Lucy and a number of other runners in the book, alongside my own experiences and tips. I have been privileged to meet some of the best athletes, coaches, personal trainers and physiotherapists through keeping fit over the years and I have included some of their expertise here too.

So what else can you expect from my guide to running? Well, in the first chapter, you'll find advice on how you can get started and a 5k training plan for beginners. You don't have to jump in at the deep end and run a marathon straight away. There are plenty of 5k and 10k races on offer so why not target one of those to get you going?

The second chapter is all about how to add variety to your training to keep you interested, and how to get fitter and faster. There's information on the variety of races you can do, and how to prepare for your perfect race and run a PB.

Dealing with an injury can sometimes be part of running so I've included a chapter with advice on how to avoid injury and how to deal with it should something happen.

I love my food and aim to eat healthily as I'm aware of how important nutrition is to running well. So information on the best foods to complement your training, along with an insight into my daily diet, is provided in the Food For Fuel chapter.

Then there's a whole section Just For Women, covering topics such as dealing with your time of the month, how to keep running while pregnant (should you want to) and how to ease back into exercise safely after having a baby. Men are of course still welcome to read this section – it might help you understand what we're going through!

Finally, if it's the marathon you're targeting then chapter six is for you. There's information

RUNNING JARGON EXPLAINED

Throughout the book there may be some common running terms you might not have heard before if you are completely new to the sport. I'll explain many of these along the way, but here's a quick guide to the basics. Later in the book, you'll find information on racing and marathon jargon, and in chapter two, there's a section covering training jargon.

PB:
Stands for personal best time – the fastest you have run in a race

5K:
A race of 3.1 miles

10K:
A race of 6.2 miles

HALF MARATHON:
A race of 13.1 miles

MARATHON:
A race of 26.2 miles

LAPS:
Referring to the track, one complete lap is 400m

REPS:
Short for repetitions, referring to running repeats of a certain time or distance in training

PACE PER MILE:
How fast you run each mile on average

RACE PACE:
How fast you run each mile when racing

on taking on the challenge of 26.2 miles, with race day tips and how I managed to achieve my aim of running a sub-three hour time. There's also a number of inspirational stories from a variety of runners who explain what tackling the long distance meant for them.

At the end of the book, you'll find a pace chart and various training schedules for beginners to more experienced runners.

The running community is growing rapidly and I hope this book will encourage even more people to become part of it by running regularly. No matter what your age, background, gender or ability, running can be enjoyed by all.

1: GETTING GOING

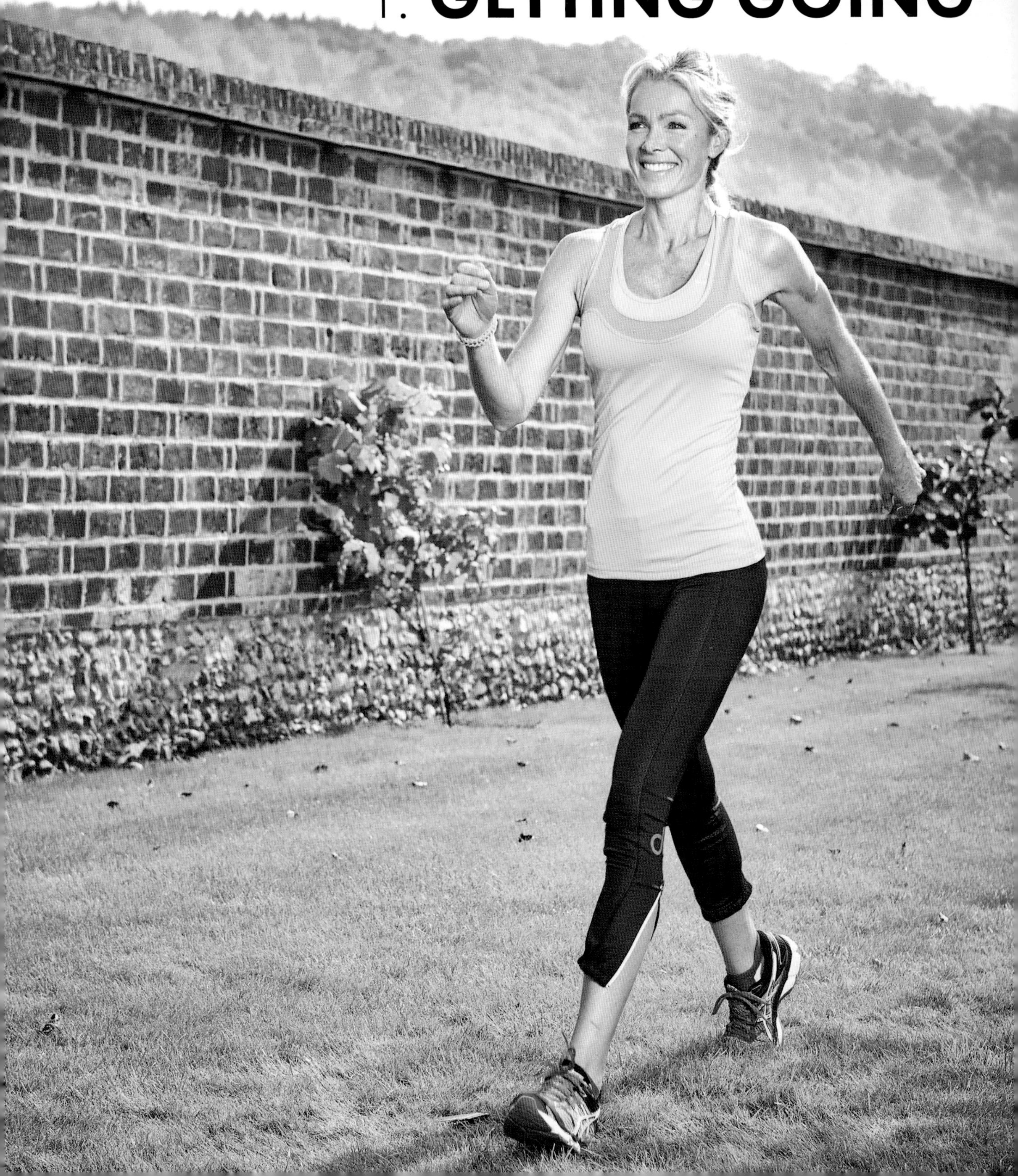

WHY RUN?

Exercise is described as a 'wonder cure' by the NHS thanks to the numerous ways it can enhance our health and well-being[1]. So why take up running over other forms of keeping fit?

Well for a start, it's one of the easiest sports to access; you don't need fancy equipment or to pay expensive gym fees. You can get up and go from your own front door whenever you feel like it. It doesn't even have to take up lots of your time. The NHS recommends 150 minutes of physical activity a week for adults[2], which means being active for just half an hour five times a week.

Running is aerobic exercise, which means it improves the efficiency of your cardiovascular system, giving you a healthier heart and lungs and better overall fitness. Studies have shown that people who run regularly are less likely to suffer heart attacks and strokes or to develop some forms of cancer. Running regularly can also reduce blood pressure and cholesterol. It burns a significant number of calories so it's also a great way to lose weight. In doing so, you are decreasing your risk of developing an obesity-related illness such as diabetes or heart disease.

Many people are concerned about the effect running has on the joints and fear it can lead to arthritis. But a 2008 study at Stanford University in the US found running can actually reduce disability in later life and help you live longer[3]. This was backed up by a study in 2013 at the Lawrence Berkeley National Laboratory, also in the US, that

HOW NICOLA WENT FROM LOATHING TO LOVING RUNNING

NICOLA KUKUC, 36, from Carlisle shares her truly inspirational story. Nicola says...

'My earliest memory is cheering on my father as he took part in the Great Cumbrian Run. I promised myself I would run it one day. However, I wasn't sporty at school so the dream of running a half marathon became a laughable memory.

'In my early thirties, I decided it was time I got fitter and entered the Cumbrian Run for motivation. I hired a personal trainer and started off walk-running. As the weeks went by, I improved but I had no confidence in my own ability.

'During the race, my trainer was by my side the whole way offering encouragement and we finished in 2 hours and 16 minutes. After the initial elation at achieving my goal, I then became deflated. I felt I had only completed the race thanks to my trainer.

'I soon gave up running, and due to a number of difficult events, I began suffering from depression.

'One day I was listening to a radio phone-in about depression when snooker champion Ronnie O'Sullivan phoned in. He talked about his own battle and how running had helped. For somebody so well known to be brave and speak out inspired me. If running could help him, maybe it could help me too?

'The next day I put on my trainers and went for a run. With each step, I felt like the black cloud that had been hanging over me had lifted slightly.

I joined another gym and found a new personal trainer who helped me build up my fitness as well as my confidence.

'I decided to take part in The Great North Run 2012 to give myself another target and to raise money for a local hospice. When I started to tire in the race, thinking about those at the hospice kept me going – I was lucky to have my health and to be able to run. Buoyed by the amazing crowd, I finished in 2 hours and 27 minutes. Although it wasn't a PB, I felt elated. I had done it with my own determination.

'Now I'm a complete running convert and I regularly race. I'm never going to come first, but I've won my biggest battle – which is to appreciate life.'

Proud: Nicola with a smile on her face finishing the Great North Run in 2014

followed 90,000 runners and walkers for more than two decades[4]. They discovered that runners were half as likely to develop arthritis or need a hip replacement. They concluded that: 'Running significantly reduced osteoarthritis and hip replacement risk due to, in part, running's association with lower BMI (Body Mass Index which is a measure of body fat).

So it's been proven time and again that running gives you a stronger, leaner and healthier body – but that's not all. Running benefits your mood too. Exercise causes your brain to release more endorphins – a 'feel good' hormone that can mask pain and create a sense of well-being. No wonder I always feel in a better mood and like I can take on the world after a run! As a result, numerous studies have found exercise can reduce the symptoms of depression and increase your self-esteem. Due to all these benefits, Dr Juliet McGrattan, a fellow columnist at *Women's Running* magazine, recommends running to her patients. She told me:

'Our bodies were designed to run and when we utilise their potential it feels good and benefits all the systems in our body. The power running has to improve our physical and mental health should not be underestimated. It gives the whole body a real workout in a short space of time and the benefits continue long after you've put your running stuff in the washing machine. I think it's particularly beneficial to people with mental health problems and those needing to lose weight, but everyone can gain from getting their trainers on.'

Juliet practises what she preaches and is a keen runner herself. She told me she runs, 'because it makes me a better person. I'm calmer, happier and can deal with what life throws at me. It energises me

and I love feeling fit and strong. Life without running is simply not as good!'

I know exactly what Juliet means as I feel the same way. As a mother of two, I love the freedom I get by going for a run. It's my 'me time' when I can clear my head, focus on myself and completely de-stress for half an hour or so.

Running has also enhanced other areas of my life. Through training and racing, I have met so many different people and visited lots of interesting places.

At races you line up with runners from a range of backgrounds and ages whom you may never have crossed paths with otherwise. I've made many friends through running and met so many wonderful and inspirational individuals.

Running has taught me how to be disciplined, dedicated and strong. It's helped me achieve feats I never thought I was capable of. I used to love watching the London Marathon on TV but I never thought I could do it – let alone in under 3 hours. I've felt proud and relieved every time I have finished a marathon, but I love pushing my body to see what I can do in an attempt to beat my previous times. This is why running really is for everyone – you don't have to be fast enough to win the race, but you can still get a massive sense of achievement just from finishing or trying to better your PB.

Alongside my sporting achievements, running marathons has enabled me to raise thousands of pounds for worthwhile causes thanks to the generous people who have sponsored me.

So as you can see, running has benefited my life in so many different ways, I can't recommend it highly enough!

WHY DO YOU RUN?

HERE'S WHAT MY TWITTER FOLLOWERS SAID

It's a great way of staying fit and setting a good example for my little girl *Steven Bird @ stevebird78*

I run for 'me' time, for my health and for chats with my running buddies *Wendy Roper-Knight @wendyrknight)*

I run to be physically and mentally strong, it's free therapy *Lou Jones @ LouHJones*

I'm an older mum so I run to keep myself mentally and physically fit – more important now than ever! *Sharon Wellings @Shazza88*

I run to challenge myself both physically and mentally, and of course to eat chocolate and drink wine guilt free! *Dawn Churm @Churmo*

Morning runs prepare me for the day ahead while runs after work clear the mind *Sara @Saras_Beauty*

I love the new challenges every time you run as well as the social side *Christopher Hastings @Hastings125*

For me there is no better way to stay fit and healthy in body and relaxed in mind. Running is its own reward *Steph Prince @Sprincie*

It's mental white noise – the only time my mind is not thinking 15 things at once *Stephanie Dales @SDales1*

I run because I can. I might not be the most graceful or quick, but just try and stop me! *PudsPost @PudsPost*

Running makes me feel amazing. Now I am a mum, it gives me some much-needed time out to clear my head and hear something other than 'The Wheels on the Bus' *Tanya Leary @MumaLeary*

I just love the feeling of running. Simple *Tracy Tibson @tracy7gibson*

AND SOME PROS

'Whether you've just taken it up or have been doing it for years, running will change your life. You'll be fitter and feel better for it, you'll find yourself chasing personal goals, and you'll have fun with other runners. Running is a bug, but one of life's good ones.' *Richard Nerurkar, Olympic Marathoner*

'I started running at school and took it more seriously when I realised it was something I was good at – I liked the feeling of winning! But of course, it's the taking part that counts and it's

wonderful to see thousands of people taking part in the Great North Run and London Marathon every year striving to achieve their personal goals – whether that's a fast time or just making it to the finish. As I always say, if you can't be first, be second. If you can't be second, be third. In other words, be as good as you can be.' *Brendan Foster, Olympian turned BBC Sport commentator*

'I run because it seems the most natural thing in the world to do. Even though I'm a lot slower now I'm usually at my

happiest when the trainers are laced up and I'm out on a long run! I guess it's what I was made to do'. *Steve Cram MBE, BBC Chief Athletics Commentator, Olympic silver medallist and World Champion*

'I run because I enjoy it. I love the feeling of running freely, especially through beautiful scenery and forests. I love the time to think (or just not think about anything) and to clear my head.' *Paula Radcliffe, women's marathon world record holder*

HOW TO GET STARTED

So hopefully by now I've convinced you to take up running, so how should you get started? Well, as I said before, it is as simple as pulling on your trainers and heading out the door, but there are some steps you can take to make it an easier, more comfortable and enjoyable experience. It's amazing how small things make a big difference, from the right sports bra to your socks.

RUNNING FORM

We're all unique, with different heights and stride lengths, so your running style will be personal to you. But there are some techniques you should try to follow whatever your physique to ensure your running action is fluid and efficient.

When you start out on those first running steps, try to stay relaxed. Don't hunch your shoulders or clench your fists into a tight ball, stay loose. Keep your head high and don't lean too far forwards or backwards. Keep scanning the path ahead to avoid trip hazards, but don't look down at your feet.

Your arms should be at a 90-degree angle to your body, let them swing forwards and back – not across your chest – in the rhythm of your run. For long-distance running don't worry about driving your arms too hard – this technique is more beneficial for sprinters trying to run at their top speed. For endurance running, it is better to be efficient and not waste energy by driving your arms – save this for your sprint finish to the line!

The same goes for your leg lift, you don't need to bring your knees up too high but do create enough leg lift so you're running and not shuffling your feet along the ground. Try not to overstride by pushing your leg too far forward as this will affect your cadence – this refers to how many times your feet hit the ground per minute when running. The optimum is 180 foot strikes per minute. If you overstride, you will make fewer foot strikes per minute and your forward momentum will be slower, even though you are working harder by using more energy to propel your foot forwards. Aim for your foot to land beneath your hip rather than in front of your body and then you will become a more efficient, and thus faster, runner.

Your running form may not feel natural at first, but remember practice makes perfect so keep at it. This also applies to your breathing. At first you might find you're gasping for breath, but your body will soon adjust and your breathing will regulate as you get fitter.

FOOTWEAR

One of the best things I ever did was invest in proper running trainers and socks. There are numerous websites on the Internet where you can buy trainers. There's so much choice and it can be trial and error to find the best style and fit. So if you're looking for your first pair, it's always best to go to a specialist running shop – such as Sweatshop, Run and Become, or Pure Running – where you can try them on. Their knowledgeable staff will be able to help you decide which trainers are best for you based on how often you intend to run and what your goals are. I've always found the staff at my local Sweatshop an invaluable source of advice on the best shoes for me.

Many shops also offer 'gait analysis', which means they will briefly watch you running (sometimes on an in-store treadmill) in order to

determine your running style so they can suggest which shoes would suit you best. They are likely to explain how you are a 'neutral' runner or one who 'over-pronates'. This refers to how your foot hits the ground when you run. The foot of a neutral runner will hit the floor evenly, while an over-pronator's foot will roll excessively inwards. Trainers for over-pronators compensate for this by having extra support, motion control and cushioning.

In the last few years there's been a new trend for barefoot running – running in minimalist shoes that encourage your foot not to land on your heel first. You can read my thoughts on that in the box below.

When it comes to the fit of your trainers, make sure there is plenty of room around your toes to avoid blisters and damage to your toenails. You should have about a thumb's width between your big toe and the end of the shoe. You might want a shoe that is half a size larger than you would normally wear, but if your foot starts to slide around when you run, it is too big. There are also trainers with different width fits which are useful if you have narrow or wide feet. Make sure they aren't too loose or too tight at your heel as this could also cause blisters. They should feel snug but shouldn't pinch.

Like any shoes, you may need to wear them a few times to 'break' them in, so never race in a new pair of shoes before you have tested them out on a few runs to ensure they are comfortable. Try the shoes on in your running socks as that will also influence how they fit and feel.

You might want to bear in mind the terrain you will mostly run on when buying trainers and consider having a separate, lighter pair for faster training sessions and races. I switched to racing in a lighter pair of trainers (also known as flats) in 2012 and I'm sure that helped me shave some valuable seconds off my times! In fact, some experts believe you can save 1 second per mile in racing flats compared to heavier trainers. It might not seem like much if you are starting out but it could make all the difference if you're going for a PB.

If you plan to run off-road and don't want winter weather like rain and snow to disrupt your training, invest in some trail shoes. These give better grip on mud and snow and some are even waterproof to help keep your feet dry. If you don't want to buy a separate pair of trainers, you could get some 'ice grips', sold at most outdoor shops such as Millets, for when it's cold and icy. They are outer soles with studs in that you can wear over your existing trainers. They are popular with walkers and mountain hikers, and brands such as Yaktrax (www.yaktrax.co.uk) do versions especially for runners.

More serious runners on the track and cross-country circuit also have 'spikes'. These are lightweight training shoes that give a better grip on synthetic tracks, grass and mud. The spikes screw into the soles of the shoe so you can change the size depending on the terrain. Track runners wear very short spikes while cross-country runners wear sizes varying from 9mm to 18mm, depending on how muddy the course they're running on is.

When it comes to socks, I've found those designed with runners in mind are the most comfortable and better for avoiding blisters. So again, it's best to buy a pair from a specialist sports shop or online. My favourite socks are made by Thorlos (www.thorlos.com).

You might have seen elite runners such as Paula Radcliffe running in tightly-fitted long socks pulled up to the knees. These are compression socks designed to aid performance and recovery. They are said to work by increasing blood flow to the muscles. You can also get compression clothing, from T-shirts to leggings. However, it's not been proven conclusively that people who do wear compression clothing run better as a result. Some studies have, however, shown they can aid recovery when worn after exercise and many wearers attest they feel better when they train and

THE BAREFOOT DEBATE

Barefoot running has really taken off in recent years thanks in part to the book *Born To Run* by Christopher McDougall. Barefoot advocates argue our bodies haven't evolved to run in trainers and the bulky cushioning they offer is altering the way our foot falls when running – leading to many common injuries. They say we are supposed to land on our forefoot to make running more efficient, but cushioned trainers cause us to land on our heel.

Embracing barefoot running doesn't necessarily mean throwing out your trainers altogether, but instead donning minimalist shoes that have little cushioning and support.

The only time I've ever enjoyed running barefoot is on a sandy beach while on holiday. The thought of doing it on the streets and parks at home doesn't appeal to me. I don't like the idea of running without any cushioning and without having adequate protection I'd worry about hurting my feet on things like sharp stones. I've also been lucky enough to find trainers that suit me really well – I train in Asics Gel-Nimbus and race in the lightweight Adidas Adizero – and have never had any major injury problems so far.

While barefoot running is said to reduce injury because it means reverting to a primeval, natural running style, some studies have found it can actually increase your chance of injury. Converts can suffer from sore calves and Achilles tendonitis, while a study at Brigham Young University in the US in 2013 found it can increase your likelihood of getting a stress fracture in your foot. So when it comes to my own training, I am of the opinion, if it ain't broke, don't fix it!

If you do decide to try barefoot running to see if it will help you stay injury-free or run faster, consider that it's not just about changing to a less cushioned pair of trainers but also about altering the way in which you run. You have to learn how to run landing on your forefoot, rather than with your heel first. This is not a technique that can be learnt overnight. You should build up your training in barefoot shoes gradually and can expect to experience some muscle pain in your legs as your body adapts.

You should also avoid doing all your training on hard road surfaces when barefoot running. Hit the trails and grassy areas instead so you're landing on a softer surface to minimise the shock impact to your body.

race wearing them[5]. So again it can be a case of trial and error and seeing what works for you personally.

CLOTHING AND USEFUL RUNNING ACCESSORIES

I'm not brand loyal so I like to mix up the running clothing I use. That means my wardrobe is full of kit from Nike, Adidas, Do Running and Sweaty Betty among others. I prefer to go for comfort over style, but running clothing is becoming a lot more stylish these days so you can have both.

When it comes to the upper body, T-shirts and long-sleeve tops made from breathable, technical fabrics are better than cotton as they draw sweat away from the body and are more lightweight. As discussed above, you can also get compression clothing.

You can generate a lot of heat running so it's important not to overdress. I often wear layers I can peel off as I warm up. When racing, I prefer to wear vest and shorts but when training, unless it's really hot, I'll keep my legs covered in leggings or three-quarter-length trousers. Lycra leggings give you a better range of movement when running than jogging bottoms, but they can be unforgiving. So if they make you feel self-conscious, layer shorts over the top.

When it's really cold, you can wrap up in thermal running tops, hats and gloves. I recently tried out some kit from Zaggora that makes your body heat up more when you're working out so it's brilliant for winter training on cold and frosty mornings. Running in trail shoes can give you extra grip if you intend to run even if it snows, as explained earlier in the footwear section.

My personal kit essentials

If it rains, waterproof, lightweight running jackets and gilets are available to buy. Ones made with Gore-tex are great at keeping your body dry. Make sure whatever waterproof top you choose is also breathable so you don't get too hot and clammy. I know it can be hard to face going out for a run in the rain, but with a good waterproof jacket you will stay dry and may even find it an exhilarating experience! It's also a good idea to wear a baseball cap to keep the raindrops out of your eyes and face.

Pulling on a baseball cap is also useful on really hot days for shielding your face from the sun and for keeping your hair out of your face. Of course, another way to do this and reduce the glare in your eyes is to wear sunglasses. Make sure you get a pair from a running or outdoor shop that is specially designed to be worn during activity so the sunglasses don't bounce on your face when you run. The other benefit of running in sunglasses in the summer is that they keep pesky flies out of your eyes.

18

In short, there's really no excuse not to go out for a run as there's kit available to aid you and make it possible whatever the weather!

Women should buy a sports bra that fits well. Being supported makes all the difference to comfort and performance. In a well-fitted sports bra, you shouldn't feel any 'bounce' from your chest so you can focus on your running form instead.

Women who don't wear a supportive running bra can get sore and aching breasts during and after running. Many large-breasted women are put off running altogether because it can be too painful, but brands like Shock Absorber and Panache do larger cup sizes so this needn't be the case.

Some sports shops offer bra fittings to help you

find the best fit. It should be snug but not too tight and shouldn't ride up at the back. You can choose from crop top styles or traditional back fastening sports bras. I prefer to wear both for extra support. If you are running a long distance, it's advisable to put lots of anti-chafing gel, such as Vaseline, under the straps of your sports bra so it doesn't rub.

It's worth wearing a sports bra whatever your size to protect your assets from sagging. Breasts do not contain any muscle and the movement of exercise can cause the breast tissue and ligaments holding them up to sag. So if you want to keep yours perky, make sure you always run with adequate support!

If you plan to incorporate running into your commute, then a running rucksack is a wise investment. They are designed to make running with a bag more comfortable so they have wider and more cushioned straps than a standard back pack. They have also been designed to sit on the back in a way that reduces the amount the bag will bounce up and down when you're running; some have straps that attach around the chest and waist to further reduce this movement. They are often made from lightweight materials so they aren't as heavy to carry.

Keeping your bag as light as possible when running is a good idea so you don't get a sore back and shoulders – so only pack the essentials. For instance, if you are running home from work and back again in the morning, you could leave your work shoes at the office and then just run with a change of clothes in your bag.

Bum bags are another useful way to help you carry what you need on the run. On most runs, you shouldn't need to carry more than your keys and perhaps a little money in case of emergency. Running shorts and leggings often come with zip-up pockets to hold such small items. But if you are going for a long run or taking part in a long-distance race, you might want to use a bum bag to store your energy gels, mobile phone, music player, anti-chafing gel etc. Again, only carry the essentials so you're not weighing yourself down and you might want to liberally apply the anti-chafing gel around your waist first so the bag strap doesn't rub as you run. Some running shops also sell belts designed just to carry water bottles and energy gels, which you might find more comfortable to wear than a bum bag.

GADGETS

You don't have to time your runs, but if you want to know how long you've been running for, any watch, stop watch or timing device (such as on your mobile phone) will do. However, if you want to get more serious and track how far you've run and at what pace, get a GPS watch. These have the ability to link to satellites so they can track the distance and speed of your run. I didn't get a GPS watch till 2012 but it changed my life! I finally knew how long some of the routes I'd been running for years were and what pace I was running per mile. One of the most popular brands of GPS watches for runners is Garmin. This is the GPS product I prefer, and I currently have their Forerunner 110. The various models come with different features and costs vary. I went for this particular model because it can display all the information I need – the length of time, distance and pace of my run – all on one easy-to-read screen.

During the marathon in 2012, this really helped me control my pace so I didn't go off too fast at the start – which was tempting as I felt really good in the first mile! When I saw on my Garmin that I was going 30 seconds quicker than my target pace to run sub-three, I slowed down. Otherwise I might have burnt out by 18 miles and struggled to finish.

A GPS watch has many benefits in addition to giving you a clear idea of how you're running. Hi-tech versions have useful features such as a virtual training partner, which you can set to run at the pace you want (it will beep at you if you go at a different pace); and you can also set up timed interval sessions during which the device will beep to tell you when to work hard and when to rest.

Most have good memories too, storing all the data so you can review your training afterwards and log it in a training diary. For those of you who love technology, you can download all the stored runs on to a computer and create spreadsheets and graphs of your training and view your routes on a

map. You can even upload this information online to share what you're up to with other people or help other runners discover your favourite route.

A heart-rate monitor is another gadget that can aid your running performance. Of course, you can measure your heart rate yourself by feeling for your pulse and counting the beats per minute, but this isn't easy when on the run! A heart rate monitor can give you the reading even when you are running at your top speed. Using one involves wearing a strap around your chest that monitors your heartbeat, sending a reading of the beats your heart is making per minute to your watch, so you can tell how hard your body is working at different paces. Many find this a useful way to increase fitness by ensuring they are working to their maximum in speed sessions. If weight loss is your goal then heart-rate monitors are useful as they can provide a more accurate figure of the number of calories you've burnt during each run.

If you are feeling unwell or are pregnant, you can also wear one to make sure you're not pushing your body too hard. Your heart rate may be higher than usual if you are unwell because your immune system is working harder to combat illness. By regularly wearing a heart-rate monitor, you will notice if your resting heart rate is higher and the beats per minute may be higher, than usual on an easy run. This could be a sign that you are becoming run-down and means you could benefit from taking it easier for a few days to recover. Note, the average resting heart rate for an adult is between 60-100 beats per minute, but it will be lower if you are fitter. Some elite athletes have a resting heart rate of 40 beats per minute. The best time to get an accurate measure of your resting

maximum heart rate, take away your age from 220. However, this method doesn't take into account a variety of personal factors, so if you do intend to train using your heart rate as a guide then make sure you follow the instructions which come with the watch to work it out accurately.

If, for example, your maximum heart rate is 190 beats per minute, you should only push yourself near this in hard interval sessions and during races – and not during every run. When working at your maximum heart rate, you will be running as hard as you possibly can, you won't have the breath to hold a conversation and your muscles will feel fatigued. So you should save this kind of effort for doing interval/speed work and when giving it all you've got in a race, such as when pushing yourself to go faster in the last mile. You won't be able to sustain this effort throughout a long race like a marathon.

On easy runs, your heart rate should be slower, at around 60 per cent of your maximum (so about 114 beats per minute if your max is 190). On runs during which you want to run faster but not flat out, for instance tempo/threshold runs, your heart rate should be about 70 to 80 per cent of your max (around 150 to 170 beats per minute if your max is 190).

Polar is a brand that makes heart-rate monitors that are popular with runners and have some good information on using one on their website www. polar.com. I haven't worn one personally, but I know lots of runners find that using one aids their training and racing. Once again, it's about finding what works for you and how you train.

heart rate is to take it when you first wake up.

When pregnant, wearing a heart-rate monitor is a good way to ensure you're not pushing yourself too much when your body is already working hard to produce a new life. Always seek medical advice before you start running while pregnant.

Some GPS watches come with heart-rate monitors included. Everyone's maximum heart rate is different and you should adhere to the manufacturer's instructions on how to work out yours. For a very rough calculation of your

WHERE TO RUN

One of the joys of running is that you can usually go out wherever you are. Wherever you live you should have a variety of options available to you. Try not to stick to the same old circuits every time. Although it's good to revisit circuits to see if you're progressing by getting round faster or with ease, you'll quickly get bored – variety is the spice of life as they say!

Not only that, you'll also get different physical benefits depending on what surface you run on. It's simple to plot different routes along roads where you live. On some days you could run out for a designated amount of time and back again and on others run in a loop.

The benefits of road running include having a firm surface, which will help you get into a continuous running rhythm. Street lighting means you can get out after dark, which could be your only option if you're at work during the day. However, try to avoid doing all your runs on roads as pounding the hard concrete surface all the time could make you more likely to get an injury such as shin splints (see more about what this is and how to prevent it in Chapter 3).

Running on softer surfaces such as grass, sand and trail routes is kinder to your joints and it will also strengthen your muscles and core as they have to work harder to keep your body stable. But watch out for tree roots and be careful where you place your feet on uneven surfaces to avoid twisting your ankle.

Local parks are great places to run traffic-free, as are canal, lake and riverside paths. Finding off-road routes will add variety and interest to your runs, whether it's an old railway track that's been converted into a footpath, a coastal path or a countryside route.

Running on an athletics track is a good idea if you want to do interval sessions so you can accurately measure how far you are going on each repetition. The surface is firm and flat so you can run as fast as you can and they are often floodlit so you can still train after dark. You might have to pay a fee each time to use the track depending on who owns it. Alternatively, you could join a running club, which usually have set evenings a week when they have exclusive use of a facility.

If you're a member of a gym, you can also do some of your runs on a treadmill. This is useful on days when you really can't face running outside when it's cold, wet and dark – however I learnt it's no fun to do all your running on a treadmill. When I was younger, I often used to run for half an hour on the treadmill at my gym at the time in Halifax – Fitness First. One of the personal trainers there, Andrew Wiggins, would always rave about the local running routes and eventually tempted me out on some of their off-road group runs. I'm so grateful to him as he was absolutely right – it's so much more exhilarating to run in the great outdoors. If you're not sure what options are available to you, check an Ordnance Survey map for your area as this will have accessible off-road paths marked on it.

If you're not lucky enough to have off-road routes, parks or beaches on your doorstep, it's worth driving to them for occasional runs to give yourself a change of scenery and terrain under foot. Websites such as mapmyrun.com, running clubs and ramblers' societies are also good sources for finding running routes. Thanks to more runners wearing GPS watches and sharing their routes online, you might also find some local runs this way. So get exploring!

STAYING SAFE

When it comes to staying safe on the run, it's all about common sense. If you're running on the roads, keep your wits about you and watch out for traffic. If there is no pavement, such as if you are running along a country lane, stick to the Highway Code, which advises keeping to the right-hand side of the road so that you can see oncoming traffic. Keep close to the side of the road and run in single file if you're running with friends. The Highway Code states when approaching sharp turns, 'it may be safer to cross the road well before a sharp right-hand bend so that oncoming traffic has a better chance of seeing you. Cross back after the bend.'

If you are running after dark, invest in some fluorescent hi-vis, reflective clothing so drivers can always see you. You could also buy a head torch if you are running after dark in an area without adequate street lighting to keep the path ahead of you well lit so you can see where you're going and avoid any trip hazards.

Many people find listening to music helps them pass the time when running so they have a more enjoyable experience. An upbeat track may help you get into the right mindset to run well and encourage you to settle into a running rhythm. However, if you do choose to listen to music while running outside, remember to be extra vigilant about your surroundings, particularly if crossing roads. Many running headphones have been designed for people to wear at the gym and so block out background noise. If you want to wear headphones for outdoor running, stay safe by getting ones that don't fully cover your ear canal or that haven't been designed to block out

background noise – then you will still be able to hear traffic or someone approaching you from behind. Adidas and Yurbuds are among brands who have designed headphones specifically for outdoor running that allow some background noise to still be audible.

Personally, I prefer not to listen to music while running outside as it's my thinking time. It's nice to

DEALING WITH COMMON RUNNERS' PROBLEMS

HOW CAN I AVOID GETTING A STITCH?

Stitches are often caused by exercising when you haven't adequately warmed up or from not leaving sufficient time between eating and drinking and going for a run. This causes a pain in the side of your stomach and can take the pleasure out of a training run or cost you a good performance in a race. To avoid it, don't eat a big meal less than 2 hours before running and avoid snacks within the hour prior to exercising. We are all different, so finding out what foods don't agree with you before running can be a case of trial and error. Drink little and often rather than gulping down a big glass of water before you run (read more about when and what to eat and drink before running in Chapter 4).

Always warm up before trying to run faster. If you do get a stitch and are able to stop, try walking it off or bending over to touch your toes. If you don't want to stop because you are in a race when a stitch occurs, try taking some deeper breaths and slowing your pace slightly. I find massaging my side with my fingers can help. Some say raising your arm above your head can help get rid of it.

HOW CAN I PREVENT CRAMP?

Cramp can be a painful experience as it causes your muscles to spasm and tighten. It's thought to be caused by dehydration and loss of salt and is common in long-distance runners. Make sure you drink an adequate amount before, during and after a long run or race and take on more fluid than normal if it's a hot day and you're sweating a lot. In a marathon, this might mean you need to take on sports drinks and energy gels too to replenish your salt levels. Strike a balance though as drinking too much could give you a stitch – it's best to drink little but often throughout a long run.

If cramp does strike, try massaging the area to relieve the pain.

BLISTERS – TO POP OR NOT TO POP?

Blisters are pockets of fluid that are formed when skin has been damaged in order to protect it. Many people find popping blisters can relieve the pain, but this also means they are more likely to become infected (if you really must pop, always use a sterilised needle). It's usually better to leave blisters to heal naturally as your skin will slowly reabsorb the fluid and the skin will then dry out. In the meantime, you can cover them with a plaster to stop them rubbing and being painful and you should avoid wearing the shoes that caused the blister until it has healed.

If you can avoid getting a blister altogether it's even better – make sure you wear shoes and socks that fit properly so they are less likely to rub and apply anti-chafing gels to areas where you are prone to blistering, such as around the toes.

hear the sounds or peace and quiet of the world as I run by. During a race I prefer to be able to take in the atmosphere and hear the cheering crowds and bands along the route. It's also not a good idea to become reliant on listening to music while running as some races ban participants from wearing headphones. This is again for safety reasons as it means runners may be unable to hear the instructions of marshals. If you want to gain the benefits of running to an up-tempo track without the dangers of headphones, you could try singing a song in your head instead!

Another important safety point is not to run to isolated areas if you're going out alone. If you're trying a new route, plot it out on a map first so you know where you're going and you don't get lost. Some GPS watches have a 'get me back' feature, which is useful if you don't have a good sense of direction. The watch will have plotted your route on the way out so when you turn back to run the same way, it will guide you along the route you took, telling you when to turn.

It's rare to get into serious trouble on a run but should something go wrong, it's best to be prepared. Always tell someone your intended route and how long you plan to be out for, so they can raise the alarm should you fail to return. If you're going on a long run, it's a good idea to carry some money (a note will easily fit into zip-up pockets on your running gear and won't weigh you down) just in case you get into difficulty. For instance, if you pull a muscle, the money could be useful for the bus ride home, or if it's a hot day and haven't had enough to drink, you could buy a drink when passing a shop. Carrying your mobile is sensible if you're worried you might get lost or can't carry on and need to phone home to be rescued. I would advise turning it off or keeping it silent though so you're not interrupted by calls or emails while running – after all it's meant to be a time to help you get away from it all!

It's also sensible to carry some sort of identification and a warning of any allergies you suffer from when running and racing. You can buy wristbands and shoe tags (which attach to your laces) that can be personalised to contain this information. When racing, write your personal details – including any allergies and medications you're taking, and a number for your next of kin – on the back of your number so the emergency services are better equipped to help you should it be necessary.

WARM UP, COOL DOWN & STRETCHING

If you've never run before, it's best to start off by incorporating periods of walking in your run. As you get fitter, you can reduce the amount of time you walk so eventually you should be able to run continuously. A lot of beginners make the mistake of trying to go too fast and then soon get puffed out. So when you do these walk-runs, the run sections don't need to be a sprint – a gentle jog is better. It doesn't matter if your pace is really slow, at this stage you just want to get your body used to running. As your form and fitness improves, you can then think about going faster.

Regardless of how fit you are, it's always important to start a run gently (known as warming up) either with a brisk walk or jog (depending on your fitness) and then pick up the pace after a few minutes' movement. Warming up is an important way to avoid an injury such as a pulled muscle as it eases your body into a run, preparing it for physical activity. It literally warms up your body temperature and your muscles by gradually increasing your circulation and heart rate.

At the end of your run, a warm down (also known as a cool down) is also helpful to alleviate muscle soreness after a run. You can ease the pace back down in the last few minutes of your run or finish with a brisk walk.

An important element of a warm down is stretching. This will increase your flexibility, alleviate muscle tightness and reduce your chance of injury. It's best to stretch at the end of a run when your muscles are still warm. Not all runners find the need (or the time) to stretch after every run, but the American College of Sports Medicine recommend stretching at least twice a week[7].

Here are some examples of stretches you can do. Stretching should be slow and controlled, you should be able to feel the stretch in your muscle with what's described by many as a warming sensation – stop if you feel any sharp pain and don't push your muscles beyond what is comfortable.

Quad stretch

Stand on one leg, bring the foot of the raised leg up behind your bottom, pull your stomach in and hold for 30 seconds. Change legs and repeat.

Hamstring stretch

Sit on the floor with your legs parted straight out in front of you. Keeping your back straight, lean forward to rest your hands on the floor between your legs. Hold this pose for 30 seconds, then reach for each foot in turn (or as far as your lower leg if you can't touch your foot), holding the stretch each time for 30 seconds

Calf stretch

Take a step away from a wall then lean forwards
into it with one leg in front of the other with your
arms pushing into the wall. The front leg should
be bent while the back leg is straight so you can
feel the stretch. You can also do this without
pushing into a wall by holding the stance as you
stand upright with one leg in front of the other,
making sure you are positioned so your knee is
over the foot of the forward leg. Then repeat with
the other leg forward.

Groin stretch

Sit on the floor and bring your feet together with
your legs bent. Gently push your knees towards
the ground and hold for 30 seconds.

Glute stretch

Sit on the floor with one leg
bent as if going to sit cross-
legged. Now bring your other
leg over to the other side of the
knee of your crossed leg. Use
your arm to hold the bent
upright knee and pull it in
towards your body, hold for 30
seconds. Repeat with other leg.

Arm and shoulder stretch

Stand up straight and raise your arms above
your head. Bend one arm behind your head so
the palm of your hand rests on the top of your
back between your shoulder blades. Bend your
other arm so it rests on the bent elbow of the
opposite arm. Hold for 30 seconds. Repeat with
other arm.

WHY DO I FEEL SO SORE AFTER A RUN?

**If you're new to running, it's normal to experience
'delayed onset muscle soreness' (DOMS) the next day.**

This is because your muscles aren't yet used to running and have been put under stress. As you get fitter, you won't feel like this after every run, but you will still get DOMS after sessions, races and long runs when you've pushed yourself harder than usual. Many athletes actually welcome this feeling as it is physical proof they have worked hard in a session or race which, in turn, will help them get fitter and stronger.

You can reduce some DOMS by stretching after a run and refuelling with protein (see more on this in Chapter 4). If you are experiencing DOMS, you shouldn't push yourself again in training that day, but do a gentle recovery run, or cross train by swimming or cycling. So if you are following a training schedule, you should avoid planning hard sessions, your longest runs or a race on successive days; build in recovery runs too.

WHEN DOES IT GET EASIER?

I know running is not easy when you first start, but trust me, you will improve and feel fitter if you stick with it. I remember when I first started jogging in my twenties, I would struggle to do a couple of miles. At first I couldn't manage to do 15 minutes continuously without gasping for breath and having to stop. But I persisted and before long I was able to do 30 minutes with ease.

It's been the same every time I have tried to push my body to run further and faster (particularly trying to get fit again after giving birth) but with persistence and patience I've got there – and you can too. You'll never know what you're capable of until you give it a try.

Everyone is different so there's no definitive answer to how long it will take for your fitness to improve when you first start running or resume training after a long period off exercising. There are a number of influential factors including your natural ability, age, general health and how often you train.

Never expect an overnight transformation in your fitness. Most people should see an improvement after six to eight weeks of consistent training. Rest assured, the more you run the easier it will become but you do have to be patient and keep going – even if at first you don't feel like you are making much progress. Remember, consistency is key – you can't run for a couple of days one week and then do nothing for a fortnight and expect to improve. Stick with it regularly and it will get easier.

FITTING RUNNING IN TO YOUR LIFE

'I don't have time' is a refrain I often hear from people who would like to run but don't. I know it's not easy if you are juggling family life with a stressful job, but even making time for half an hour a couple of times a week will make all the difference to your health and well-being.

Think about your daily routine and when you could fit it in. Could you get up earlier and go first thing? Could you sacrifice half an hour of TV viewing to go in the evening? If you're a parent, could you literally do a school run? You could walk to school with your child and then run home. This was one way I fitted the miles in when I was marathon training and taking Devon to and from school. Then after Anya was born, I ran with her in the running buggy to pick Devon up, balancing his scooter on top of the buggy. Then I ran home again while he scooted beside me.

If you're a commuter, could you run to or from your workplace or get off the train or bus a stop earlier to run the rest of the way?

Joining a running club can make a big difference – could you set aside one evening each week to attend a club session?

If you're a dog owner, then your pet can make a fantastic training partner. Since you have to go out to walk it anyway, why not run? Lucy often runs with her dog and she has the following advice:

'I do most of my runs with my border collie, Patch. He's excellent company as he's always full of energy and enthusiasm (even on the days when it's pouring with rain). Working and pastoral dog breeds such as collies, spaniels, huskies and Labradors make better runners than other breeds so if you are choosing a dog as a training partner, make sure it's a breed that's built for running. Remember to build up their training gradually as you would your own and don't run with them on

My best friend Zoe didn't take up running until she was 40. She joined her local voluntary club, Skelton Run England group, as a way to lose weight and get fit with her teenage daughter, Kennedy

very hot days as they don't sweat like humans do, instead cool off by panting. It's best to get a harness for your dog so the lead attaches over its back rather than to a collar around its neck, as then it won't pull as much, strain its neck, or have any difficulty breathing. You can also get your own harness that attaches around your waist with a clip for the dog's lead so you can then run with your hands free. You can even take part in races with them, such as parkruns and Cani-cross events (visit www.cani-cross.co.uk for more information).'

Once you have fitted running into your routine it will soon become a habit, making it more of a pleasure and less of a chore. But don't beat yourself up if you can't go running every day – aim for quality over quantity if you are pushed for time.

Lucy running with Patch

HOW TO STAY MOTIVATED

PLAN AHEAD

At the start of each week, think about what you have on each day and when it will be possible to fit in a run. If you plan to run at a certain time you're more likely to do it. You might need to arrange to get up earlier one day or organise your kit so you can run home from work etc.

RUN WITH A FRIEND

Team up with a friend or relative so you can support and motivate one another to go for a run. If you've arranged to meet someone you'll be less likely to back out if you don't feel like it as you'd be letting them down. Running with someone else also helps the minutes tick by faster as you can have a good gossip as you run.

KEEP A TRAINING DIARY

Keeping a log of what runs you've been doing will help you see the progress you're making and how far you've come. You can look back on the runs you've done with pride and look forward to building on it as you get fitter and faster.

JOIN A RUNNING CLUB

You'll never be short of people to run with if you join a club and attending once or twice a week will help you get into the habit of running regularly.

ENTER A RACE

Planning a race gives you a goal to aim for and adds focus to your training. This definitely worked for me when I signed up for my first London Marathon. Once I entered I knew I had to put the training in so I didn't let down myself, or the charities I was raising money for.

GET COMPETITIVE

You don't have to aim to win an Olympic medal but setting yourself targets will help you stay motivated. You could aim to complete a race in a certain time or finish ahead of a certain person. This will spur you on in your training.

REMEMBER WHY YOU RUN

Maybe you're running to lose weight, to raise money for charity or to improve your health. Whatever your reason, keep it in mind when a little voice in your head tries to convince you to forgo your run and stay in watching TV instead. If you stay committed, you'll reach the target you're striving for.

My BMF instructors, 'Curly' Dan and 'Nice' Nick. They may look friendly but they push you to train hard!

BEGINNERS' 5K TRAINING PLAN

Whether you are a novice or a more experienced runner looking to increase your training, it's important not to do too much too soon or you could make yourself ill or cause injuries. You should always increase your mileage gradually – by a maximum of 10 per cent per week – so your body can adapt to the increase. Even if you can only walk initially, you'll soon build up the distance you can run.

If you want to start running but aren't sure how often – or for how long – to run, then try the 'Couch to 5k' training schedule outlined overleaf, which has been provided by Sensev El-Ahmadi. I met Sen when I completed a Run England Leadership in Running Fitness course (which I thoroughly recommend if you want to learn more about running, or qualify to start up your own running group. Visit runengland.org for more details). Sen set up the 'How We Run Club' in North London and has helped hundreds of people to get active.

Members of Sen's club who have followed the training schedule below have been able to run a 5k time trial after six weeks. Remember, consistency is key – you can't run for a couple of days one week and then do nothing for a fortnight and expect to improve. Stick with it regularly and it will get easier. So why not try it yourself, find a 5k near you that will take place in six weeks' time (such as a parkrun) and follow the schedule in the build-up. If you don't feel ready to race at that point, instead do your own 5k time trial at the end of the six weeks by measuring out a course with a GPS watch, using your car to measure a route on the roads or plotting a 5k course with the help of a website such as mapmyrun.com.

Sen guides and encourages her running group to do their best

COUCH TO 5K

	DAY 1	DAY 2	DAY 3
WEEK 1	Walk for 2 minutes, then jog for 2 minutes. Repeat 5 more times. Total workout time: 24 minutes	Walk for 2 minutes, then jog for 2 minutes. Repeat 5 more times. Total workout time: 24 minutes	Walk for 2 minutes, then jog for 2 minutes. Repeat 5 more times. Total workout time: 24 minutes
2	Walk for 2 minutes, then jog for 3 minutes. Repeat 4 more times. Total workout time: 25 minutes	Walk for 2 minutes, then jog for 3 minutes. Repeat 4 more times. Total workout time: 25 minutes	Walk for 2 minutes, then jog for 3 minutes. Repeat 4 more times. Total workout time: 25 minutes
3	Walk for 2 minutes, then jog for 3 minutes. Repeat 5 more times. Total workout time: 30 minutes	Walk for 2 minutes, then jog for 3 minutes. Repeat 5 more times. Total workout time: 30 minutes	Walk for 2 minutes, then jog for 3 minutes. Repeat 5 more times. Total workout time: 30 minutes
4	Walk for 1 minute, then jog for 3 minutes. Repeat 7 more times. Total workout time: 32 minutes	Walk for 1 minute, then jog for 3 minutes. Repeat 7 more times. Total workout time: 32 minutes	Walk for 1 minute, then jog for 3 minutes. Repeat 7 more times. Total workout time: 32 minutes
5	Walk for 1 minute, then jog for 4 minutes. Repeat 6 more times. Total workout time: 35 minutes	Walk for 1 minute, then jog for 4 minutes. Repeat 6 more times. Total workout time: 35 minutes	Walk for 1 minute, then jog for 4 minutes. Repeat 6 more times. Total workout time: 35 minutes
6	Walk for 1 minute, then jog for 4 minutes. Repeat 7 more times. Total workout time: 40 minutes	Walk for 1 minute, then jog for 4 minutes. Repeat 7 more times. Total workout time: 40 minutes	**5k Race**

HOW ANDREA BECAME A 5K RUNNER IN JUST SIX WEEKS

ANDREA CHAPMAN, 49, from North London, followed the couch to 5k schedule. Here, she reveals how she got on...

'I signed up for the Couch to 5k programme with the How We Run Club after making a New Year's resolution to get fit.

"The first week was tough. It was January, so it was cold and the routes around the park were muddy and slippery. By the end of each run I was tired and my legs ached. But by week three, I started to feel fitter and my running form and breathing improved.

'When the length of the runs increased in week four, it proved a real challenge. Not just physically, but fitting it into my day. I could have easily given up but I stuck at it and by the end of week six, I was ready for the 5k time trial.

'When I woke up that morning, I felt nervous with butterflies in my stomach. When I got there, it was great to see everyone I had been training with and I sensed they were all as anxious as I was. This is what we had been working towards over the last few weeks.

'As I started the race, I worried that I wouldn't be able to make it. I knew I had to pace myself so I settled into a running rhythm that felt hard but sustainable.

'As the minutes ticked by, it became harder but I kept telling myself to keep going. Finally, I reached the end and was relieved to be able to stop. My heart was pounding and it was hard to catch my breath. I felt nauseous with heavy legs. Then the realisation of what I had achieved sunk in. I had just run 5k in 31 minutes and 32 seconds on a hilly, off-road, route. The feeling of accomplishment washed all the pain away, I was euphoric!

'My advice to anyone thinking of taking up running is DO IT! It's a fantastic way to improve your fitness, meet new people and challenge yourself. You can follow the Couch to 5k programme on your own, but I would recommend joining a local running group like I did or doing it with a friend.'

For more information on the How We Run Club visit www.hwrc.me.uk, follow @sensevruncoach and @hwrc1 on Twitter, or like their Facebook group at www.facebook.com/hwrc1.

Achievement: Andrea, right, with coach Sen after completing her first 5k

2: GETTING FITTER

Once you're able to run continuously for half an hour or more, you could start to add some variety to your training by doing different types of running workouts. Not only will this make your training much more varied and interesting, it will also help you become fitter, faster and stronger.

If you want to increase your speed and fitness and get quicker PBs then you need to improve both your lactate threshold and V02 max. This can be done through interval sessions, tempo runs and runs during which you raise your heart rate, as explained in this section. You can mix one or two of these types of sessions into your running routine each week. However, make sure you intersperse hard training days with easy ones (or rest days) to avoid illness or injury.

INTERVALS

Interval training involves running harder (for example at your race pace) for a set amount of time with brief periods of jogging in between to get your breath back. You can do various repetitions depending on your fitness and which race distance you are training for.

 I used to do interval training with my running club, but now I have two children I can't make it to their evening sessions, so I do intervals on my own, timing myself with my watch. Interval training is definitely the best way to get a hard workout from running as it raises your heart rate and teaches your body to run faster.

Interval sessions are an effective way to enhance your lactate threshold. Lactate is a chemical that builds up in your muscles when you exercise hard as it is a by-product produced by the muscles as they convert fuel for energy to maintain a fast pace or effort. When you have a lot of lactate in your muscles, you will start to feel pain and discomfort and struggle to go any faster despite pushing yourself to the limit – coined by some as 'feeling the burn'. This is the threshold of your lactate threshold. You can increase this point by regularly doing interval training as part of a training routine.

Such sessions will also enhance your VO2 max. VO2 max refers to the optimum rate at which your body can use oxygen during exercise. The higher your VO2 max, the faster you will be able to go.

An element of it is genetic, which is why if the average person did the same training as an elite athlete like Mo Farah, they still might not be able to keep up with him. You might have noticed this when you train with a friend and find they improve at a faster rate than you do or vice versa.

Your VO2 max is also influenced by your age and gender. While there are limits to everyone's VO2 max, you can still improve yours and run to the best of your ability by regularly doing speed work.

So if you want to be able to go faster for longer in a race, interval training is the answer. Aside from improving your speed, if weight loss is your goal, these types of sessions will help you burn more calories because they boost your metabolism (read more on this in the running for weight loss section of the Food For Fuel chapter). They work on the same principle as High Intensity Interval Training classes (HIIT) as you are working hard for a period of time and then having a short recovery.

During the intervals, you should be pushing yourself so your heart rate is high and you get out of breath. However, you also need to pace yourself so you can complete the whole session – so don't go too crazy on the first rep! The fitter you get, the better you will become at pacing your efforts. But

EXAMPLE INTERVAL SESSIONS

I'm grateful to two-time Olympian and Commonwealth medallist, Liz Yelling, for supplying the following sessions.

If you're new to interval running, you may need to reduce the number of reps at first or extend the length of recovery. Pick your target distance, then do the recommended sessions once a week in training (and variations on the same time and distance) and this should fire you to a PB!

If you're not sure what your race pace is, refer to the pace chart at the back of the book.

When sessions are given in distance, e.g. 5 x 1k, you can run them on the track for an accurate measurement or if you have a GPS watch, use it to measure 1k. If you cannot measure the distance, run for the equivalent time it would take you to cover 1k at your target pace instead. For example, in the case of a 25-minute 5k runner doing the first 5k session below, they would take 5 minutes to run 1k so they should do 5 x 5 minutes with 2 minutes recovery.

5K

a] 10 mins easy warm-up; 5 x 1k at race pace with 2 mins walk/jog recovery; 10 mins cool-down.

b] 10 mins warm-up jog; 200m hard, 200m jog x 15 (or 40 secs hard, 40 secs jog x 15); 10 mins cool-down.

10K:

a] 10 mins warm-up; 5 x 2k at race pace with 2 mins jog recovery; 10 mins cool-down.

b] 10 mins warm-up jog; 12 x 90 secs as fast as you can with 90 secs jog recovery; 10 mins cool-down.

HALF MARATHON:

a] 15 mins warm-up; 12 mins steady (faster than a jog but comfortable); 12 mins at target half-marathon pace), 12 mins as fast as you can; 15 mins at 10k pace or cool-down.

b] 15 mins warm-up; 1 min, 2 min, 3 min, 4 min, 5 min, 4 min, 3 min, 2 min, 1 min with 2 mins jog recovery between each rep; 15 mins cool-down.

MARATHON:

a] 15 mins warm-up; 15 mins at marathon pace followed by 2 mins jog recovery; 5 x 3 mins at half marathon pace with a 90 secs jog recovery between each rep.; 2 mins jog recovery, followed by 5 x 45 secs hard, 45 secs walk recovery; 15 mins cool-down.

b] 15 mins warm-up; 3 mins at marathon pace, immediately followed by 3 mins faster than marathon pace (i.e. a faster pace you can maintain for the whole session) x 10; 15 mins cool-down.

Liz Yelling runs a sports coaching consultancy with her husband Martin. They can provide bespoke training plans for runners of all abilities. For more information visit www.yellingperformance.com

whatever your fitness, an interval session should never be easy! If it is, you're not working hard enough and need to increase your speed.

The day after, it's normal to have achy muscles (DOMS) so don't do hard sessions like this on consecutive days if you intend to do them more than once a week.

You should also do a warm-up and warm-down jog of at least 10 minutes before and after the sessions. The warm-up will prepare your body for the speed work while the warm-down will reduce muscle soreness afterwards. The warm-up and -down will also increase your daily mileage, but because it's broken up with the session, you can cover a number of miles without even noticing it.

FARTLEK

This comes from the Swedish word 'speed play' and as its name suggests it's a good way to incorporate going faster within runs while having some fun with

it! It's basically an unstructured interval session as it involves going for a run during which you go at different speeds and intensities throughout.

You can decide when you run harder – and how long to run harder for – as you go along. For example, you might decide to run harder for the distance between three lamp posts and then ease off or run harder as you go up a hill. You can also use your watch and run harder for a set amount of time during the session.

It's completely up to you, so you can make it up as you go along and run how you feel. Make sure you are fully warmed up before doing any increases in pace though to avoid pulling a muscle.

HILL REPS

Running uphill is great for strengthening your legs and improving your stamina. Find an uphill stretch near you and stride up as fast as you can. Then jog back down and go again. You could do a set number of reps or just run up and down for a certain amount of time.

PAARLAUF

This word means 'pairs' in German so it's a session for which you'll need a partner. It gives you an opportunity to do an interval session and raise your heart rate but, as you're working with someone else, you can support and motivate one another.

The format is like a continuous relay, whereby one of you works hard while the other rests and you swap places when you hand over. There are various ways you can do this. For example, you could run out and back for a minute while your partner jogs on the spot where you started. When you return, your partner then runs hard out and back for a

44

minute while you jog on the spot. You can repeat this procedure until you've both done a set number of hard reps.

A paarlauf is traditionally run on a 400m track, with you and your partner both starting at the 150m point on the home straight. One of you then runs hard anti-clockwise round the track while the other runs across the centre of the track to the opposite side on the back straight. When the former reaches the latter, the two runners swap roles – the person who has been running hard will stop and jog across the middle of the track back to where you started. The other will start running hard on the track round the next bend till you both meet at the 150m mark on the home straight again and swap again.

You can repeat this for a certain length of time, e.g. 20 minutes or until you've both run a set number of hard efforts round the bend.

TEMPO, AKA THRESHOLD, RUNS

This is when you run at a harder pace than usual for a sustained period or distance. If you're aiming for a 5k, you should aim to complete a tempo run of at least 2 miles, while serious marathon runners will do tempo runs for 10 to 15 miles.

You should feel like you are running faster than on an easy run (it will be hard to hold a conversation at this pace), but it shouldn't be a flat-out sprint. It should be at about 70–80 per cent of your maximum effort; about 30 seconds slower per mile than your fastest pace.

These types of runs are great for helping you learn what pace you are capable of sustaining. They also burn more calories and help you become more efficient at running at your race pace so it will feel easier on race day.

STRIDES

Strides can refer to a broad range of running drills that can form part of a warm-up before a speed session or race. They are most beneficial for sprinters and middle-distance runners as they help them to focus on their running form and improve their cadence (the number of times the foot strikes the ground per minute when running).

Strides are usually done for about 50m to 100m and can include running with an exaggerated knee lift (aka high knees), or running kicking your legs back so your heel touches your bum each time (aka heel flicks).

Strides also include literally striding out at a faster pace – close to your top speed (so almost sprinting) – for up to 100 metres. Done after a warm-up jog, but before an interval session or race, this procedure can help to prepare your body for running at speed.

So if you want to incorporate strides into your running, try doing a few drills before an interval session (for example, do each of the following drills over 50m with a jog back to where you started in between each rep: 2 x high knees, 2 x heel flicks, 2 x sprints). Alternatively, you could do a couple of sprint strides towards the end of an easy run to help improve your leg turnover and speed, or incorporate them into a fartlek. Just remember to always do a warm-up jog before embarking on strides to avoid pulling a muscle.

LONG RUNS

These are a must when you are marathon training to get you used to the time you will spend on your feet covering 26.2 miles. They're also important to non-marathon runners – although you won't need to run as far.

Generally speaking, a long run just means you run for a longer amount of time than normal. So if the maximum time you run for in the week is 30 minutes, a 45–50-minute run will be long for you. Marathon runners will do long runs of 2–3 hours.

A long run improves your endurance as it teaches your body how to use stored energy as fuel, so it can keep going for longer. It should be run at an easy, conversational pace.

Since it will take the most time out of your day of all your runs, most people (and training schedules) fit the long run in on weekends.

DO I NEED A COACH?

This very much depends on how seriously you want to take your running and how self-motivated you are. Coaches are an invaluable source of advice for elite runners and help them to reach their full potential. This isn't just by pushing them to train hard, but also by advising them when it's necessary to back off and take a break.

Coaches are great at motivating you and giving support and guidance and can supply you with a training programme that will help you peak for a certain race. I have never had a running-specific coach, but I have benefited from working with personal trainers over the years, including Jim McDonnell (pictured right), Matt Church and Darren Anderson, who have been fantastic at pushing me to work harder and advising me on how to get fitter and stronger. Just a few sessions with each of them has taught me different things, which I have been able to take on board and build upon.

If you feel your running would benefit from having the structure and support a coach would provide, then seeking a qualified expert at your local running club is the best place to start. Many running clubs will offer general coaching advice to all members and will have qualified coaches overseeing sessions. It's worth enquiring if they would be able to coach you personally.

As I mentioned earlier in the book, Run England operate a Leadership In Running Fitness course which I have undertaken. Leaders are qualified to organise

running groups and can offer lots of useful advice on getting started and getting fitter. To find a Run England group leader near you, visit www. runengland.org.

There are also numerous experienced experts who offer online coaching, such as Liz Yelling and her husband Martin at www.yellingperformance.com

My main man, Jimski. I ran the London 10k with Jim McDonnell, aiming to go sub 40 but missed out by 10 seconds!

JOIN A RUNNING CLUB

I can't recommend joining a running club highly enough. They can boost your confidence and are the best places to get advice and support. There are hundreds of athletics and running clubs around the country, which are almost always open to new members.

Some are 'athletics clubs' who cater for sprinters, jumpers and throwers, as well as middle- to long-distance runners, while others are purely jogging/running clubs that focus on fitness and running longer distances. See which clubs are available in your area and ask if you can join them for a training run. Most clubs will allow you to join in for a few sessions before deciding if you want to become a full member and will always extend a warm welcome to potential members.

Annual membership should be a fraction of the cost of joining a gym. Being a member of a running club could actually help you save money as you can get a discount on entry to many races and some running shops give discounts to club members. Many clubs also compete in road and cross-country league races that members can take part in for free.

If you are after a coveted London Marathon spot, being part of a running club could also help you with this. Clubs in the UK are offered a certain number of places each year depending on the number of members. How these places are allocated is down to the clubs themselves, but some hold their own ballots or will ask members to apply for the places.

As a member of a club, you'll get to meet new people and learn from the expertise of the coaches and more experienced runners. This will not only help you improve but it will also help keep you motivated – I've always found chatting to people who share my passion for running puts a spring in my step and increases my desire to train. It could also enhance your social life as many clubs will arrange pub outings and parties.

Most clubs organise group runs at certain paces which you can join in with so you don't have to run alone. This will help the miles pass quicker and give you a chance to take routes you might not usually run on. In addition, many will hold weekly track or road interval sessions you can join. It's so much easier to get through these sessions when you have other people around to keep you going.

When it comes to racing, being part of a club gives you the opportunity to experience team spirit in what is not a traditional team sport. Many clubs participate in national relay races, while at certain events, including the London Marathon, there are prizes up for grabs for the fastest teams.

However, some of you may be thinking 'I'm not good enough to join a club'. It's a common misconception that running clubs are only for serious athletes and Olympians – in fact it's one I once held myself. I felt very apprehensive about going along to my then-local club, Thames Valley Harriers, for the first time but it proved invaluable to improving my fitness.

My friend, Alison Tingle, who was already a member, always raved about how fantastic the club was so she suggested I go along to help my training after I agreed to run my first London Marathon in 2004. I wasn't sure at first, but eventually I plucked up the courage to go along and try it out one dark, cold Tuesday evening.

I ran a few Saturday mornings with Honley off-road running group. We usually ran about 10 miles followed by eating fried egg sandwiches and lots of cake! From left: Paul Coleman, Richard Makin, Dick Facey, me, Christine Couch and behind, Jonathon "Trout" Trollope

As I was driving there I felt apprehensive and I thought about turning back and going home. But knowing Alison was waiting for me, I carried on. She met me at the gate and we went into the clubhouse together to meet the middle-distance runners who I would be training with. They were all so welcoming and friendly, I soon felt at ease. They were all delighted about having a new recruit and their enthusiasm made me keen to get started on that evening's track session – a 'pyramid' session. This consisted of increasing the distance of each rep until we reached 1k and then going back down again – so we ran 400m, 600m, 800m, 1000m, 800m, 600m, 400m, all with about 90 seconds' recovery in between. The idea is to run each rep as hard as you can, but pace yourself so you can complete the whole session. It hurt but I got through it and I was overjoyed.

I kept going back every week. Sometimes we would do pyramid sessions, other times we would do mile reps or 400m repeats. It was always hard work but the variety of doing different distances made it more interesting. I'd always still be a little bit nervous on the drive there about the pain that was in store, but I always left feeling fantastic and fitter. I'm certain I wouldn't have improved my marathon times if I hadn't joined a club.

Running clubs aren't just for adults, most clubs take children from the age of 8–10 (read more about getting children into running in the 'juggling running and parenting' section in Chapter 5). I sometimes wish I had joined a club when I was a youngster – who knows what I may have achieved then!

To find a club near you, search British Athletics' online directory at www.britishathletics.org.uk/ grassroots/search/

LUCY'S EXPERIENCE OF RUNNING CLUBS AS A CHILD, STUDENT AND ADULT

LUCY shares how running clubs can enhance your training and relationships...

'Thanks to my Dad, Roy, being a talented runner (with a marathon PB of 2 hours 39 minutes), my older sister, Amy, and I grew up thinking running was the norm.

'When we were old enough, we joined him as members of our then-local clubs, Altrincham AC and Sale Harriers. I was only about eight so I wasn't conscious I was exercising but just enjoyed running around having fun. As we got older, the sessions became more structured and we started competing in cross-country and track races.

'I then went to Loughborough University and joined their athletics club. Loughborough is renowned as one of the best universities for sport in the country so I was never one of the fastest but there was a great team spirit. I felt proud to compete in the Loughborough vest and this pushed me to run as hard as I could – as a result I started to improve.

'Through the athletics club at university I made many friends who remain among my best friends today. We went to races together, abroad on training trips and met for long Sunday runs at 10 am after dancing till 3 am the night before (I'm not sure how we managed that now!).

'After leaving university, I moved closer to London and joined my local running club – St Albans Striders.

'It was daunting going to the track session for the first time, but like Nell's experience at Thames Valley, I didn't feel alone for long as the other club members were friendly and welcoming. Being part of the club helped me feel more settled after I had moved to a new area and I now count many of the members among my closest friends. It's also how I met my partner, Ed, so if you're single, consider running clubs a great place to find love!

'Being part of a running club as a child, teenager, student and adult has enhanced my health and lifestyle in numerous ways. So don't be shy about joining your local club, you've got a lot more to gain than you have to lose.'

Lucy, left in both pictures, with some of her running friends

50

CROSS TRAINING TO ENHANCE YOUR RUNNING

If you want to be a better runner, you don't just have to run. Over the years, as well as running, I have loved doing other forms of exercising too, such as boxercise and Body Pump classes and lifting weights.

More recently, I've loved joining in at a British Military Fitness class at my local park. It's an outdoor group fitness class during which you do shuttle runs, burpees, press-ups, sit-ups, etc, so it's a real all-body workout that's hard work but lots of fun, I thoroughly recommend it (visit www.britmilfit.com for more information).

If, like me, you like to do different types of exercise, then you don't need to sacrifice these

BMF is a great way to keep overall strength, fitness and motivation going all year round. I have loved being part of this team

workouts for running. Every bit of exercise that you do counts towards making your body stronger, fitter and healthier, which will enhance your athletic ability. Not only that, different sporting activities such as swimming and cycling are excellent ways to supplement your training as they give your body a break from the impact of running while still working your muscles and making you out of breath. Meanwhile, strength and weight training, as explained below, can make you a stronger runner and help prevent injury.

STRENGTH AND WEIGHT TRAINING

In my Peak Energy Recharged workout, we do a number of moves that are beneficial for runners, such as balancing on one leg to improve ankle strength and squats and lunges to produce stronger leg and bum muscles. Obviously I recommend doing the DVD (available from Amazon and other stores) for a full weekly workout, but if you don't have time, you can still incorporate some strength work into your weekly running routine by doing some of the moves in this section after – or during – a run. For example, on a run you could use a park bench to do tricep dips and step-ups.

Tricep dips

For tricep dips (which are great for banishing bingo wings!), sit up on the edge of the bench with your legs extended. Place your hands palms down on the bench on either side of your hips. Move your bottom forwards off the bench and slowly lower yourself down and then push back up and repeat 10 times – without resting your bottom back on the bench each time you lift up. Build up till you can do three sets of 10.

Step-ups

For step-ups, simply find a step or raised ledge (like a park bench again) and step up on it with one leg, bring the other leg up and then step back down again. Repeat 10 times in a running action so you're doing it with a little speed, and then swap so the other leg is stepping up first.

Exercises like these and lunges, squats and press-ups, for which you use your own body weight as resistance, are a simple but effective way to tone up – as well as being convenient and free. You could do sets of the above every week at the end of a run and it will only take up a few extra minutes of your time.

Lunges

For lunges, stand tall then take a big step forwards with one leg, keeping your back straight, and then lower your body to the floor till your front leg is at a 90-degree angle and the back leg is bent and low to the ground behind it. Push back up to standing and repeat 10 times, then do it again on the opposite leg. If you have space, instead of pushing back to standing, you can push forwards and keep doing the lunges in one direction rather than on the spot. You can also do jumping lunges – whereby you spring up into the air in between each lunge – to increase the workout. Another option is to rest your back leg on a step or bench (as pictured) and bend up and down.

Squats

For squats, start by standing up straight with your feet shoulder-width apart and your hands on your hips. Bend your knees and lower yourself down with your hips and bottom positioned as if you were going to sit on a chair. Keep going until your thighs are parallel with the floor, then push back up to the standing position and repeat 10 times, building up to three sets of 10. If you want to make the move more energetic, add a jump as you push back up to the starting position.

Press-ups

For press-ups, start by lying straight, face down on the floor with your palms positioned on either side of your chest. Then push up with your arms until they are straight and your body is raised so you are balanced on your toes. Slowly lower your body back down, without resting your whole body on the floor, the push up again and repeat 10 times, building up to three sets of 10 as you get stronger. Personal trainer Stuart Amory (who is great to follow on Twitter @StuartAmoryPT to motivate your fitness regime) recommended the Runtastic PushUps App to me, which is a useful tool for tracking your progress – you'll go from barely being able to do one press-up to doing dozens with ease. If you are struggling to begin with, try resting on your knees instead of your toes, as shown below.

TRY THIS WORK OUT

See the explanations on pages 51–53 for how to do the following moves and then do the routine after or during a run twice a week to become fitter and stronger. Try to time these sessions so they don't fall on the same day, or the day after, you have done a hard run or session.

Do each of the moves continuously (i.e. 10 squats without stopping), and move straight on to the next exercise. If you need to, take 30 seconds recovery between exercises:

10 x squats (and/or jumping squats to increase the workout)

10 x lunges (and/or jumping lunges to increase the workout)

10 x tricep dips

10 x press-ups

If you are fitter, repeat the circuit three times with a 30 second recovery between each circuit (if you are super fit, you might not need the recover).

If you have dumbbells and want to increase the effort, hold them while doing the squats and lunges and add 10 x bicep curls after the press-ups.

DON'T BE AFRAID TO PUMP IRON

Strength training has really helped me run faster in the past. When I trained for my second London Marathon, I trained once a week with former professional boxer Jim McDonnell, who has run a 2 hour and 50 minute marathon (read more on how we met in the marathon chapter). I met him in a boxing gym and he had me doing shuttle runs, squats, press-ups and boxing on pads. It was an exhausting but effective all-body conditioning workout. I don't think he was expecting to see me again after that first sweat-busting session, but I'm a glutton for punishment and returned every week!

Each time he would have me running up and down stairs with weights and doing as many squat thrusts and press-ups as I could manage. On one occasion he even had me running around a field pulling a tyre that was fastened to me with a rope round my waist. It's all the stuff he puts boxers through before a fight to help them become physically and mentally prepared for the ring.

The hard work paid off when I ran the marathon that year as I achieved a time of 3 hours and 10 minutes – a PB of 12 minutes at the time. It was this that made me realise what I can achieve when I push my body to the limit and it was the first time I

realised I might be capable of a sub-three hour time with the right training.

Many men incorporate weight training into their running regime – Mo Farah credits it for helping him become a double Olympic champion. However, lots of women think weightlifting is not for them. Let's erase this myth – women, you can weightlift and it won't result in you looking like a bulky bodybuilder. It means you'll be more toned and have a stronger and fitter body. As discussed later in the book in the 'running as you age' and 'running and the menopause' sections, weightlifting is also important as we get older as it can help keep the bones stronger.

As well as Jim, I have also worked with other trainers over the years, including Darren Anderson and Matt Church, who have taught me the importance of weightlifting and how it can enhance my running ability. I worked with Darren before the marathon in 2012 and he taught me how to use an Olympic bar (a weighted bar) to do snatches and cleans (movements that involve you raising the bar from the floor and then over your head). Once these moves are mastered, you can get an Olympic bar and do them at home. Doing this kind of weight training gave me a strong body ahead of my 90-mile-a-week training plan. However, I didn't keep up the weight training during the 12-week marathon build-up this time as I didn't have the time or energy. Instead, I just did strengthening exercises such as squats and press-ups.

After I had recovered from the marathon in 2012, I resumed some weight training, this time with Matt at Locker 27 (www.locker27.com). They do workshops on how to lift weights correctly and circuit training with battle ropes and tyres. Doing

such workouts gave me another focus after concentrating on long-distance running and it was fun to do something different to high mileage while still keeping fit and strong.

I thoroughly recommend being taught how to use weights equipment like an Olympic bar by a professional before you try them yourself because, if used incorrectly, they could do more harm than good. Contact a personal trainer in your area or one at a local gym for their advice. Joining a gym is a great way to get started in weight training – even if, like me, you don't remain a member once you have learnt the moves and are confident doing them at home (and are able to afford equipment such as an Olympic bar at home).

Another way to start off doing some weight training at home is to buy a set of dumbbells. Start with a weight as low as 1kg and use heavier ones as you get stronger. Bicep curls are easy to do and will give you shapely and toned arms. Start with the dumbbell in your hand by your side and bend your arm, bringing the weight up to your shoulder and then slowly lower it down again, repeating 10 times (you can build up and do two more sets of 10 as you get stronger, and then use a heavier weight as it becomes easier). You could also progress to lifting the weights from shoulder height to straight up over your head and back down again. Again, on my Peak Energy Recharged DVD, we do a short 'heavy hands' workout led by Liam Duffy doing various moves using dumbbells – I recommend following this to learn some techniques so you can join in with our class at home and don't feel like you are working out alone. You can also do the squats and lunges explained earlier while holding the dumbbells to increase the intensity.

CORE STABILITY

Another set of exercises you can do at home to give you a stronger body is core stability moves. The core refers to a group of muscles in your torso. The core muscles are around your abdomen and back and are commonly likened to a corset because of the way they can pull your stomach in and improve your posture.

A strong core is important for runners as it can enhance your balance and stability and decrease your risk of injury. It also helps give you a flat stomach and we all want one of those!

Plank

The most effective core exercise is the plank. Lie face down on the floor and then prop yourself up so you are balanced on your forearms and toes. Your back should be straight and your stomach muscles held in. Remember to keep breathing. Hold this position for 30 seconds. At first you might struggle to hold it and find yourself wobbling and your muscles complaining, but it will get easier. As you get stronger you can then do more repetitions or hold it for up to 90 seconds. You can also make it harder by balancing on just one leg and raising the other.

Side plank

A variation on this exercise that will work the muscles on each side is to do a side plank. As the name suggests, you should start by lying down on one side. To do the right side first, position your right elbow under your right shoulder and then raise your body so your hip is off the ground and your body is propped up on your right forearm and the outside of your right foot. Focus on holding your stomach muscles in and hold this position for 30 seconds or up to 90 seconds as you get stronger. When you get stronger, you can progress to balancing on your hand with your arm straight as pictured. Then do the same on your left side.

STRENGTHEN YOUR CORE

This will only take a few minutes to do after a run two or three times a week. See pages 56–58 for an explanation of the moves and complete as follows:

Start with the plank, holding it for 30 seconds

Then do the side plank for 30 seconds each on the left and right

Now hold the pelvic lift position for 30 seconds, then raise your bottom and hips up and down 10 times

Next do 10 crunches

Finally flip from your back to your front and do the back exercise, raising your upper body up and down 10 times.

Hold planks for longer and do more crunches as you get fitter.

Pelvic lift

Another move that will also strengthen your bottom muscles as well as your core is the pelvic lift. Lie on your back with your knees bent and your feet touching the floor. Then raise your hips and bottom off the ground so your weight is on your feet and across your upper back and your body is in a straight diagonal line. Hold this position for 30 seconds. Then do a set of 10 raising your hips and bottom up and down into the position – but don't let your bottom rest on the ground each time. You can increase the difficulty by straightening one leg.

Sit ups

Doing sit ups is another effective way to strengthen your stomach muscles and core if done correctly. Start lying flat on your back with your feet on the floor and knees bent. Place your hands crossed on your chest or behind your ears (but if you do the latter, make sure you don't use them to pull your head as this will strain your neck), then slowly raise your head and shoulders up and back down again. Make sure you hold your stomach muscles tight and repeat 10 times.

Back strengthener

Finally, don't forget to strengthen your back as well. Lie face down with your arms straight out in front of you and then slowly lift your head, shoulders and feet off the floor and back down again. Repeat 10 times.

Back strengthener

THE JOY OF RACING

You don't have to take part in races to be a runner, but you'll be missing out on a large part of what makes the sport so enjoyable if you don't. Races are the times when I truly push my body to run as hard as I can and I've often surprised myself with how I have got on.

Races are also a time to join together with other runners and be part of an amazing atmosphere. At all the events I have been to, everyone has always been supportive and encouraged one another, which has spurred me on to run well.

You can't beat the feeling of crossing the finishing line either. However tired I am at the end, I always try and sprint for the finish and throw my arms in the air like I've won the whole thing! When my son sees me afterwards with my medal he often asks, 'did you win Mum?' and I reply 'I won my own race, against me!' As that's what it is – it's *your* challenge.

It's up to you how often you race. Some people just do one or two a year, others race every weekend. A good strategy to keep you motivated is to target a race for which you want to run your best and do some other races in the build-up. In the preparatory races you can practise your race plan and test your fitness over different distances.

When it comes to the media coverage of running, the marathon gets the most attention. But you don't have to run 26.2 miles in order to experience the joy of racing. There are so many different races on offer every weekend. So how do you decide which race is for you? Here's a selection of some of the many races you can take part in...

PARKRUN

I can't recommend parkrun highly enough. If you haven't heard of it by now, where have you been?! There are parkruns all over the UK and other parts of the world. They are held every Saturday morning at 9am in parks up and down the country and are completely free to take part in. All you have to do is register beforehand on the event's website and print off a barcode to take along on race day.

All the races are 5k in distance and are for all abilities and ages. You can run with your dog, with your pushchair or your children if you want to. There are also some junior parkruns, which are 2k-long and are held specifically for children aged 4 to 14 and their families.

Once you've completed the 5k run, you are handed another barcode. Both that and your personal barcode, which you took along with you, are scanned and the results are published on the parkrun website within a few hours.

The events are so successful because of the many volunteers who enthusiastically give up their time on a Saturday morning to marshal the race and scan the barcodes and they should all be applauded for the work they do.

While the event is billed as a 'timed run' rather

60

than a race, if you are a competitive person, you're still catered for. The winners are announced each week online and there is a record of achievement of those around the country who have run the fastest times. You can track your own progress on the event's website to see if you can beat your time from a previous week.

I regularly take part in my local parkrun and I love the fantastic, supportive atmosphere. They really are for everyone, so you could have a super-speedy Olympian lining up with someone running their first 5k, providing both inspiration and encouragement to newcomers.

When I was pregnant, I still took part. I ran at a slower pace and acted as a pacemaker (which means running at a set, advertised pace so people can fall in just behind or beside you if they want to run at that speed – it's like having your own human Garmin!). It was really rewarding helping people achieve the time they were aiming for.

Me and my family: I walked with my niece Abi in a baby carrier.

For more information on parkrun and to find your nearest event, log on to www.parkrun.org.uk.

RACE FOR LIFE

Another 5k series that's great for runners of all abilities (as long as you're female!) is Race For Life. It's all for a great cause – Cancer Research UK – and you can walk or run depending on your fitness.

The events are usually held up and down the country over the spring and summer and they now stage 10ks and obstacle-course races as well as 5ks. The races are for women only, which may appeal to those who feel intimidated about lining up with men.

For more on Race For Life, visit www.raceforlife.cancerresearchuk.org.

WOMEN'S RUNNING 10KS

Women's Running magazine also stages women-only 10k races across the UK in the spring and summer. I've taken part in lots of them and they are fun, friendly events for all abilities. As an ambassador for the race series, it has been a great opportunity for me to meet *Women's Running* readers and hear about them achieving their goals.

Women's Running advertise their races in their monthly magazine and on their website, www.womensrunninguk.co.uk or you can sign up at www.wr10k.co.uk.

OTHER ROAD RACES

Road races vary in length, but the standard race distances staged in the UK are 5k, 10k, 5 miles, 10 miles, 20 miles, half marathon and marathon.

There are numerous races held every weekend (and some on weekdays) so there are a few things

to consider when deciding which one is right for you.

When it comes to the length, keep in mind that running a half or full marathon requires commitment to the training. Getting the miles in ahead of race day will take up a fair amount of your time. So if you have time restraints but still want to target races, focus on shorter distances instead. This is what I had to do after my children were born. When they were really young I knew I wouldn't have the time or energy to train for a marathon, but I enjoyed doing 5k and 10k races instead.

You might also want to consider the kind of race you want to take part in. There are women-only events, novelty races (such as Santa races at Christmas, for which everyone dresses up as Father Christmas. I have done one of these and it was great fun with a family atmosphere) and big city road races.

The big city races like the London Marathon (held every spring) and Great North Run (a half marathon held every autumn) should not be missed as they are amazing both for their atmosphere and scale. Thousands of runners take part while even more people line the streets to cheer them on. There are often bands playing music on the course and runners of all shapes, sizes and fitness are involved – from elites to fun runners. I recommend all runners experience big road-running events, but keep in mind they can be more expensive to enter and unless they're local you will have additional costs and hassle in terms of transport and accommodation.

Big city races will also have a higher number of entrants so the course will often be congested. You may find you can't run at your own pace at the start because there are so many people around you, so they're not always the best places to get PBs. Smaller, local races are sometimes organised by running clubs, councils or charities. While they won't be on as grand a scale in terms of facilities and crowd support, they can provide the best opportunities to run fast times. *Runner's World* magazine have an excellent directory of races across the country on their website. Visit www. runnersworld.co.uk.

ULTRA MARATHONS

Anything over the standard marathon distance is considered an 'ultra' and they could be 30 miles, 50 miles or more than 100 miles in distance! As you are running for so long, camping overnight during the race or running through the night is sometimes involved.

Giving your body enough fuel to keep going is important when ultra running so there are 'feed stations' where you can stop for food and water.

Events like the Santa Dash keep motivation going in winter months Here I am with my friend Caryn and her daughter, Ruby

There are some super-quick ultra runners out there, but most who take part do it for the challenge of covering the distance rather than going for a fast time. So you might prefer this type of race if you enjoy running slowly and steady.

I have never done an ultra, and at the moment I would rather focus on going faster than further – but never say never!

Lucy in a cross-country race

OFF-ROAD (AKA CROSS-COUNTRY/TRAIL) RUNNING

Off-road running basically means running on a surface other than the road or athletics track, so it could be on grassy parkland, over farmers' fields or through woodlands. Off-road racing is traditionally known as 'cross-country', but is sometimes also referred to as 'trail' running.

A few decades ago, middle- to long-distance runners followed a format of racing on the road and track in the summer, then over cross-country courses in the winter. But in recent years, as road running has become more popular and road races are staged all year round, cross-country has fallen out of favour with many.

You will often only get the opportunity to take part in cross-country league races if you join a running club. There are various leagues around the country for clubs in the same region to compete in, as well as national events including the English National Cross Country (held every February since 1887) and Inter-counties Cross Country (held every March and during which athletes are picked to run for their county. This event frequently acts as a GB selection race for the now bi-annual World Cross Country Championships).

Cross-country races are generally 6–8k in length for women and 9–15k in length for men (at some events men and women run together, but usually they're held as separate races).

Taking part in cross-country races is an excellent way to experience team spirit, running for your club, as there are usually team positions at stake as well as individual honours.

Running on off-road surfaces is good for strengthening your leg and core muscles and it will

improve your stamina and stability – so it's also good training for road races. The courses are often challenging as they can be muddy and hilly, but your performance is not measured by what time you run, rather by what position you finish in. So it provides a fun opportunity to embrace the competitive side of running, forget about your pace per mile and focus on beating the person in front of you instead.

Some of the world's best road runners have taken part in cross-country races as children and adults, such as Mo Farah, Paula Radcliffe and the Brownlee brothers.

Lucy loves cross-country racing. She told me why: 'In cross-country races, you can truly experience the child-like joy of racing free from worries about mile splits and PBs. It's all about getting round in the highest position you can, while having fun charging up and down hills and splashing through mud. I recommend it to everyone regardless of their pace as it's suitable for all ages and abilities.'

FELL RUNNING

This is a more extreme version of cross-country/trail running as it involves running off-road across rugged landscapes and mountainous terrain. You might not have many fell options available if you live in a city, but you can't escape it if you live in my birthplace of Yorkshire or other hilly areas such as the Lake District.

Fell running is another good way to strength your legs – in particular your ankles – and will give you a tough core as your body needs to be able to stabilise on the uneven terrain.

Fell running will certainly give you the best

opportunity to see some breathtaking landscapes while running, but it's not for the faint-hearted! Some of the ascents and descents can be almost vertical and weather conditions can be tough.

OBSTACLE-COURSE RACES

Events such as Tough Mudder and Survival of the Fitness have grown in popularity in recent years. They are almost like cross-country racing in that you might have to run through mud and over hills, but they also throw in additional obstacles to make it more challenging. Some mirror Army assault courses so you might have to crawl under a net, wade through a stream or clamber over a wall.

OVERCOMING OBSTACLES AND REDISCOVERING THE JOY OF MUD!

Bring it on! Sarah Cole takes part in an obstacle race

I haven't taken part in one but SARAH COLE, 28, from North London, has. She told me what you can expect...

'Obstacle racing requires strength, stamina and most importantly mental grit, but don't be put off them if you're not super-fit. I would say I am of average fitness – I can complete a 5k in around 30 minutes and my record number of pull-ups is one. The good news for anyone thinking they are not strong enough is that it's such a friendly sport and helping out your fellow runner is all part of the experience. There is also a huge choice of races you can sign up to, from the 5k-Spartan Sprint to the 13-mile Spartan Beast or Tough Mudder races.

'Despite my trepidation before my first obstacle race, I really surprised myself. Instead of dreading what was coming next, I found the voice inside my head saying: "Bring it on!" Parts of the course were like an adult playground – in fact I really did feel like a child again. I was climbing, crawling, taking the odd tumble and heading straight for mud instead of going around it. There is something pretty exhilarating about that. With every obstacle I overcame, the bigger my sense of achievement, and when the finish line was finally in sight, (just obscured by the final obstacle – a fire jump, no less) I felt like I could take on anything. I would heartily recommend giving obstacle racing a go if you are looking for a new challenge or for something different to road running.

RACE JARGON

Here are some common terms you will come across when racing that you may not have heard before in relation to running...

CHIP

This is a device to accurately record individual race times. Chips usually attach to your shoelaces, or tie around your ankle or are attached to your number. Your chip is activated when you cross a mat at the start line. It is deactivated when you cross the finish line and the time is recorded.

CHIP TIME

The time your chip recorded from the race's start to its finish line.

GUN TIME

Your gun time is the time it takes you to reach the finish line from the moment the starting gun sounded. If you are in a race with thousands of people and start towards the back of the field, there will be a large discrepancy between your gun time and chip time because it could take you a while to cross the start line after the race has officially started. Only people at the very front of the field will have a matching gun and chip time.

RACE MARSHALS

These people will direct you where to go during a race, and if necessary, divert or make traffic wait, while runners pass. Be polite to them, many voluntarily do this job for no reward and can end up standing outside for hours! Pay close attention to their instructions, as they may give out safety warnings on the course, alerting you to an upcoming sharp bend or bollard in the road etc.

AGE CATEGORIES

As you age, you progress from being a 'junior', to a 'senior', and then a 'vet' (sometimes also referred to as 'masters'). 'Juniors' are competitors under the age of 20. Women up to the age of 35 and men up to the age of 40 are known as 'seniors'. Women become 'vets' at the age of 35 while for men it's 40. Once you become a 'vet', you go up a veteran age group every 10 years.

AGE GRADING

This might be shown as a percentage by your name when race results are published. It's a means of rating your performance based on your age and gender. The higher the figure, the better you performed.

SPLITS

The time it took you to run certain sections, e.g. mile splits. A negative split occurs if you run the second half of the race faster than the first half.

BLOWING UP

A phrase that means going off too fast at the start of the race and then struggling to finish.

RACE DAY TIPS

There are many ways you can prepare for a race, both mentally and physically, as well as various things you can do to help the big day run smoothly.

SLEEP WELL THE WEEK BEFORE

The night before the race, you might find you don't sleep well (I never do!) because you are nervous, or you may not get as many hours as usual if you have an early start to get to the event. So try to make sure you get some early nights in the week preceding the race and, most importantly, two nights before the race.

Sleep is when your body repairs itself so being well-rested and refreshed before the race will make all the difference to your performance.

EAT SENSIBLY

Your body needs fuel to run well so eat healthily, including lots of fresh fruit and veg in the build-up to the race.

If you're running a marathon on a Saturday or Sunday, you should eat more carbs from the Wednesday before the race, but you don't need to worry about this as much if you're racing over a shorter distance. Just have a carb-heavy meal, such as pasta with vegetables the night before. Read more about nutrition in Chapter 4.

HAVE A GOOD BREAKFAST

Don't skip breakfast on the day of a race as you'll need the fuel to get you round. Eat 2–3 hours before the run to make sure it's fully digested so you don't get a stitch or feel sick. Stick to foods you've eaten before running previously, this isn't the time to try something new. Toast with jam, a banana or porridge are good pre-race foods.

STAY HYDRATED

Exercising is thirsty work because your body loses fluid when you sweat. You need to drink to avoid becoming dehydrated, which will impair your race performance and make you feel weak and light-headed. So make sure you've had a good drink of water the morning before the race (but don't drink too much too close to the start as this could give you a stitch).

How much fluid you take on during the race is then dependent on how far you are running and what temperature it is. If, for instance, you are running a 5k on a cold day, you shouldn't need to take on a drink during the race. But if you are running a marathon, you will need to take on water little and often throughout whatever the weather, and if it's a hot day you'll need to drink extra.

You should always drink more if you're running on a hot and sunny day because you'll be losing more fluid by sweating more. But don't go overboard on pre-race fluid consumption or you'll end up being desperate for the loo when racing!

As you get fitter, you should become more attuned to your thirst. It's not very pleasant, but looking at your urine is the best way to tell how

hydrated you are. The darker the colour, the more dehydrated you are. Read more about hydration in Chapter 4.

BE PREPARED

Get your kit ready the night before – pin your number on to your vest and attach your chip to your shoelaces (if you haven't been sent your race number in advance and need to collect it on the day, don't forget to pack safety pins!). Make sure your GPS watch is fully charged if you're using one.

Plan your route to the race and allow plenty of time to get there so you don't have the added stress of running late or getting lost trying to find the start. Queues for the toilets can be notoriously long at races so you should always allow plenty of time for that (especially as nerves may mean you need to go more than once!).

Pack plenty of warm clothes for after the race and a spare pair of trainers if it looks like it's going to rain.

DON'T GET COLD

Once you've arrived at the race, been to the loo etc, then do a short warm-up jog and don't strip off too soon. I often see runners on the start line who look freezing because they've been hanging around in just their vest and shorts for too long.

If you do have to put your kit into baggage storage some time before the start, then wear an old T-shirt or bin bag to keep warm which you can throw away when the race starts. Some race organisers collect the T-shirts left at the start and donate them to charity. If you dump a bag, try to use a bin and don't leave it in the path of other runners following behind you.

START THE RACE IN THE RIGHT PLACE

Many races will have signs up telling you where to stand behind the start line depending on your predicted finishing time. Or you may have been allocated a zone to stand in when you received your number. Always adhere to this and don't be tempted to move forwards so you are closer to the start line. If a race is chip timed, it doesn't matter if you don't cross the line when the gun goes as you'll still get an accurate time from the start to the finish.

If you line up among runners who are faster than you, you can cause congestion when the race starts and have a frustrating first few miles jostling for space with faster runners pushing from behind to overtake. You could also be tempted to go off too fast trying to keep up. By starting in the right zone,

You never know who you will meet...

68

you should be among other runners of a similar fitness to you so you will be able to run at your target race pace.

PACE YOURSELF

It's always tempting to go off fast at the start as the adrenaline is pumping and it feels so easy to begin with! But you'll suffer later in the race if you overdo it. You're more likely to run a PB if you run at an even pace throughout the race or even better achieve a 'negative split' – which means you run faster in the second half. Practise your target race pace in training so you learn how it feels, or use a GPS to help you control your speed.

If it's your first race and you're not sure what your pace is, take it easy at the start and get faster if you feel up to it towards the end. This way, you'll have a much more enjoyable first race experience than if

you go sprinting off and then find it difficult to carry on. Believe me, I've been there! In one of my first races, a 10k in Leeds, I went off far too fast and then after 15 minutes I felt terrible and thought I was going to be sick. I got slower and slower and struggled to finish, ending up with a time I was very disappointed with. I knew I was capable of much better. The next time I raced, I didn't go off as fast and as a result I felt stronger throughout the race and achieved a better time.

As you can see from my experience, when you're new to racing, finding your race pace can be a real learning curve, so don't let a bad experience put you off – learn from it instead. Conversely, as you get fitter you might find you finish a race and still feel like you had more left – so then you'll know for next time that you can go a bit faster without fear of 'blowing up'.

Volunteering at a running event can be just as rewarding as racing. I was proud to be part of this all-ladies pacing team at the home of park run, Bushy Park

DEALING WITH RACE-DAY NERVES

You're likely to have butterflies in your stomach and feel anxiously excited on race day. Don't worry, this is completely normal. It's good to feel this way as it makes the event feel more special – it's not just another run.

Your body is releasing the hormone adrenaline to prepare you for the race ahead. Adrenaline can help you run better because it raises your heart rate and increases blood flow to your muscles. This is why a trainer I once worked with, Jim McDonnell, who trains professional boxers advised me: 'Invite the fear in, make it your friend'. What he means is, if you embrace your nerves you can actually use them to help you perform better. Don't worry that you have increased adrenaline as it will enhance your performance.

If you get stressed about being nervous, you might get yourself so worked up that you can't run well. Many people get too nervous because they fear failure – they worry 'what if I can't finish?' 'What if I don't run as fast as I know I can?' Again, these are all normal concerns for runners and it's good you feel this way, this desire to succeed is what drives you to train. My advice is to keep calm and focus on the positives. Think of all the training you have done in preparation and how that will help you run well. Believe in yourself. One of my mottos is 'Believe. Achieve.'

So don't let your nerves beat you before you have even started running – forget the 'what ifs...' and tell yourself 'I can do it!' (see more on the powerful impact of positive thinking in the 'mind over matter' box on p70).

Of course, things can't always go to plan and if you do have a bad run, then put it into perspective

and remember it's only a race. A below-par performance is not worth being miserable about for long. Think about what you can do to improve next time – could you have eaten better before the race? Could you have done more miles in training? Maybe you've over-trained and need a good rest? Or perhaps you had unrealistic expectations? Don't dwell on the negatives but learn from them. There will always be other races when you can try and do better.

AND FINALLY... ENJOY IT!

Be proud as you cross the finish line and get your medal, and celebrate your achievement with friends and family afterwards. Get some warm clothes on as soon as you can after finishing and have a recovery drink such as milk or a protein shake.

MIND OVER MATTER

Sometimes finishing a race or a hard training session can be as much of a mental battle as a physical one.

Here are some tips on how to harness the power of mind over matter in races...

THINK POSITIVE

Running requires willpower. If you tell yourself 'I can't do it', then you won't. So think positive and believe in yourself and what you are capable of. It can be hard to continue thinking positively as fatigue sets in. So if negative thoughts arise, give them a positive slant. For example, instead of thinking 'there's still two miles to go' think 'there's only two miles to go.'

THINK BEYOND YOUR BLISTERS!

If you're pushing yourself to the limit, you won't feel comfortable throughout a whole race. Dig in and remember what doing well will mean to you. The discomfort you feel during the race will soon be forgotten when you finish and blisters will heal – but you'll have bragging rights about a achieving a PB forever!

HAVE A MANTRA

Chanting a positive, personal mantra while running can help you stay in a rhythm and keep your mind focused. Your mantra could be a phrase, quote, or even just one word to keep you motivated such as 'run hard' or 'power'. When I ran my marathon PB, I kept repeating the phrase, 'I can do this' to keep my pace going – and it worked!

VISUALISE SUCCESS

This is a common tool used by sports psychologists to help elite athletes achieve their goals. The idea is that by imagining success in the build-up – for example by visualising the moment of crossing the finish line first or stepping onto the medal podium – it will become more likely to happen. You can also attach feelings to your visualisation to make you feel better on the day. For instance, if you are preparing for the London Marathon, visualise passing Big Ben with a mile to go and imagine feeling strong, confident and on target for a PB. Then, on the day, tap into this feeling again as you pass Big Ben.

DISTRACT YOURSELF

Sometimes running a long distance can become mentally tough because it seems so far. So find other ways to pass the time rather than ticking off the minutes in your head. For example, count to 100 or sing a song in your head. You could also try breaking the race up into different sections and focus on getting to the end of each section rather than the finish to make it seem more manageable.

HOW TISH TOOK UP RUNNING AND GOT FITTER AND FASTER

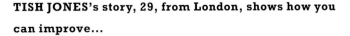

TISH JONES's story, 29, from London, shows how you can improve...

'I've always been sporty but I wasn't a great runner at school and I preferred playing team sports. There was no real decision for me to take up running for athletic gain or fitness. In my late teens, it was something I started to do for escapism because my family life at the time wasn't good and running felt like a natural way of getting away from it all.

'It wasn't until my mid-twenties that I started to train and race regularly and take it more seriously. I joined Belgrave Harriers Athletics Club, based in South London, and started competing for them in cross-country and road races. Running with others in the group sessions made me push myself harder than I did when running alone. I received tremendous support and encouragement from people at the club and I started getting faster, setting me on the path to becoming an elite athlete – which is something I'm sure I wouldn't have pursued, or even considered possible, if I hadn't joined a club.

'I have always been a hard worker and I knew becoming a faster runner would require discipline and dedication. Alongside part-time jobs, I started training much harder. Fitting the training in around a busy schedule often involves multi-tasking, but now running has become my passion so training is never a chore, I love it. In 2014, I achieved a half marathon PB of 1 hour and 12 minutes.

'I've enjoyed learning about nutrition and how it impacts performance and recovery. If you eat healthily and understand your body's requirements, you have a great foundation to run well. I include lots of protein in my diet and I can't be without my daily probiotic drink and a snack of dark chocolate.

'To anyone taking up running, be warned, you will be hooked! But don't worry, this is not a bad thing. I recommend joining a club so you're not just running alone. Also, remember to sleep well, eat well, hydrate, recover sensibly and look after your feet. Don't compare yourself negatively to other runners – a mile is a mile, well done for completing each and every one, regardless of how long it takes.'

Talented: Tish Jones is an elite athlete

When you first take up running, push yourself to run faster or do higher mileage, it's inevitable that you will start to feel some aches and pains. When you're a beginner it's hard to know when it's ok to carry on training or if you should stop. As you get fitter, you will begin to understand this better as you become more attuned to your own body. If all runners stopped every time they felt a niggle or a tight muscle they would never get any training done, so the odd ache doesn't mean you shouldn't run. Often you may find a muscle ache that you have when you start running will go away as you get warmed up. It's not unusual for the muscles to feel stiff and sore after running. You can avoid some post-exercise fatigue by stretching (see examples in the first chapter) and by ensuring you rehydrate and refuel quickly after a run by drinking water or milk and taking on protein to repair the muscles – read more about this in the Food for Fuel chapter later in the book.

3: PREVENTING & DEALING WITH INJURY

SPORTS MASSAGE

One of the best ways to alleviate muscle pain is by getting a sports massage. But please don't think from the word 'massage' that this will be a relaxing and tranquil experience! Firm pressure needs to be applied in a sports massage to release tension in the muscles – it's like being steamrollered, but afterwards you feel like a different person, I really recommend it.

A good sports masseur will apply pressure to your muscles and sometimes use their elbow to trigger point a tight area such as your glutes (your bum muscles) to release tension. So don't be alarmed if it hurts, this is definitely one of those times when the saying 'no pain, no gain' applies. You're likely to feel achy and heavy-legged the next day so don't have a massage too close to a race – I would leave at least three days between a massage and an event.

Sports massage increases the blood flow to your muscles and flushes toxins out of your body. It can be overlooked, but it should be seen as a proper treatment and better for you than taking medicines to mask the pain of aching muscles. Often you will find that an ache or niggle such as a sore knee can be solved with some sports massage.

Lucy's mother, Sandy Waterlow, is a fully qualified sports masseuse. She explains:

'Sports massage aids recovery from hard training and racing by breaking down muscle tensions. It's a great way to prevent injury and to make legs feel fresher and more flexible during heavy training periods or after a race. Elite athletes rely on sports massage to keep them in prime condition, but recreational runners can get huge benefits from regular sports massage too. Deep-tissue massage may feel uncomfortable at times and you may be a little achy the following day (it's not recommended to run hard the day after a sports massage), but the day after that you should feel like you have new legs as your muscles will be less tense and tight. Remember to always find a fully qualified therapist who specialises in sports massage rather than a general massage.'

If you are doing high mileage, you might want to consider booking a sports massage every month. At £30–50 an hour for a treatment it can be expensive to get a sports massage regularly but it's money well spent if it keeps you injury-free. A good massage will have a much more lasting and beneficial effect than a shopping spree or a boozy night out so consider if there's something you could do without in order to afford more massages.

USING A FOAM ROLLER

You can do some DIY massage yourself (or ask your partner to help you), or another effective way to self-massage is to buy a foam roller. These are hard cylinders that you put on the floor and then roll your body along to apply pressure to the muscles. Again, it should feel painful as you use it – if it doesn't you're not doing it right.

For example, if you lie on the roller on your side, you can release tension in the IT (iliotibial) band – the large sheet of fibrous tissue that runs up the outside of your thigh, connecting your knee and your hip (a tight IT band can cause knee and hip problems). If you sit and roll on the roller you can release tension in the glutes (the muscles in your bottom, which can often get tight when running giving you sore hips or an achy back). If you don't have a foam roller, you can also do the same thing using a tennis or golf ball, or a rolling pin or aerosol can will also do the job.

Here are some examples of massages you can do using your foam roller. Do these a couple of times a week after running...

IT band

Lie on your side, propped up on one arm and rest the roller under your knee. Use your arms to slowly push your body down so the roller moves up your leg, dragged along the outside of your thigh all the way to your hip. Then repeat, starting with the roller at the knee again. If you find a particularly painful spot as you roll along the outside of the thigh, hold the roller there and apply more body weight on the roller. This 'trigger points' the tension in the muscle, which will help release it. Repeat on the other side.

Glutes

Do each glute in turn. Sit on top of the roller with your weight on the side of the glute (bum cheek) you intend to massage, with your arms balancing your weight behind you. Start with the roller at the point where your bottom meets your leg and use your arms and legs to move your body slowly so the roller moves up towards your back over your bum muscle. Repeat and then do the other glute. If you have a particularly tender point in your glute, a tennis ball is a better way to massage it because it has a smaller surface area. Sit on the tennis ball and move your bottom across it. Hold the tennis ball on the tender spot and apply more body weight to release the tension – be warned, it will hurt!

Calves

Do each leg in turn. Sit down with one leg bent and the one you want to massage straight out. Put the foam roller under the bottom of the straight leg where it meets the foot. Use the other bent leg and your arms to help you drag your body forwards so the roller moves up over the calf muscle to the knee joint. Lift your body up with your arms to apply more body weight on to the muscle. Remember, it should hurt: if the roller moves without you feeling anything, you are not applying enough pressure. Repeat, and then do the other calf.

TREATING AN INJURY

As explained previously, aches and pains will often go away as you warm up when running and can be alleviated with some post-run stretching and massage. If, however, you have a persistent ache when running – or experience any sharp pains in your body – then you should stop. Making the decision to stop when out on a run can be difficult, but it could prevent more damage being done in the long term.

When I was training for the marathon in 2012, I had to abandon one of my 20-mile runs as I experienced a sharp pain in my Achilles heel. I was disappointed that I couldn't complete the run and felt defeated as I had to catch the bus back home (luckily I was carrying just enough money for the bus fare so I recommend other people do the same on long runs!). But it was the right decision as not pushing on through the pain meant I didn't make the injury worse.

If you experience pain such as this while on a run or have pulled or strained a muscle, then the best treatment to follow initially is the procedure known as RICE, which stands for Rest, Ice, Compression and Elevation.

Resting will allow your body to heal and prevent further damage. Even if you're not injured, it's important to have regular rest days during which you don't do any running, to allow your body to recover and adapt to the training you have done.

Icing helps as it can numb the area so you feel less pain, and the coldness causes the blood vessels to constrict, reducing swelling and inflammation.

Elite athletes such as Paula Radcliffe and tennis player Andy Murray believe in the benefits of icing so much they'll have regular ice baths after a hard training session in order to help their muscles recover and reduce injury. I'm not brave enough to take the plunge – I'd rather have a warm bubble bath! – but I definitely recommend icing isolated areas if you have a muscle strain or applying ice following an injury such as a sprained ankle. You can buy ice packs to keep in your freezer or simply use a bag of frozen peas wrapped in a tea towel. Ice the area for 5–10 minutes at a time.

Compressing a pulled muscle can also help alleviate swelling. You can use a bandage or don compression socks if it's a lower-leg injury.

Elevating the injured area can further reduce swelling, so if you've sprained your ankle or pulled a calf muscle you should keep it propped up when sitting or lying down. Use a footstool and cushion or keep it elevated. You can also take anti-inflammatory drugs such as ibuprofen (always take this with food to avoid stomach ulcers). Anti-inflammatory drugs are better than paracetamol in this instance as they reduce the swelling as well as alleviate pain.

After following RICE for four days, if you still see no signs of improvement, you should then seek the advice of a physiotherapist who will be able to advise you on the best course of recovery to get you running again. This is what I did when my Achilles was still sore a few days after my abandoned run. I went to see physiotherapist Sam Bishop who runs a practice called PACE Therapies with Sarah Bowen in Cobham, Surrey (PACEtherapies.co.uk). He's a decathlete and has treated many world-class sportsmen and women. He knew just what to do to treat my Achilles. He explains:

'If you are unsure of whether you are injured or just experiencing "training niggles" it is usually best to stop running for a short while, as Nell did. Missing a few runs may save you weeks of lost running at a later stage. If you are in pain, it is essential to seek the advice of a physiotherapist quickly to have any concerns assessed and diagnosed. A physiotherapist can help you identify the stretches and mobility or strength exercises most relevant and essential to you depending on your running style and training goals. If you're not sure where to find a physio, then talk to runners or members of running clubs in your area. Failing that, a request on Twitter can often link you with the right person (I'm at @PhysioSB) – word-of-mouth referrals are frequently the best. Always check that your physio is registered with the Health and Care Professions Council.'

Thanks to Sam, I was able to run the marathon weeks later and achieve a PB. So always remember to listen to your body, don't push yourself through sharp pains as it could do more damage, and book an appointment with a physiotherapist if the pain persists. An appointment with a physio can cost from £40 to £70, so if it's something you can't afford to pay for yourself, you could visit your GP and see if they can refer you to see an NHS physio. However, it may take longer for you to get an appointment this way.

WHO SHOULD I SEE WHEN I'M INJURED?

If in doubt, speak to your GP first as they can advise you or refer you to another medical professional. Take this route if you think you need further treatment such as physio but want an NHS referral.

A PHYSIOTHERAPIST

Physiotherapists are defined by the Chartered Society of Physiotherapy as 'helping people affected by injury, illness or disability through movement and exercise, manual therapy, education and advice.' They have a database of qualified physios on their website (www.csp.org.uk). For a running-related injury, it's best to visit a physio who specialises in sports injuries. As Sam says, word of mouth is often best so ask others runners at clubs and via social media who they recommend.

AN OSTEOPATH

Osteopaths study for longer than physios (four to five years for an undergraduate degree as opposed to three for a physio degree). The British Osteopathic Association write on their website that osteopaths can treat numerous conditions, but are commonly thought of as back specialists. They state: 'Osteopaths have a holistic approach and believe that your whole body will work well if your body is in good structural balance... We use a wide range of techniques, including massage, cranial techniques (sometimes referred to as 'cranial osteopathy') and joint mobilisation, and this breadth of approach allows us to focus on every patient's precise needs.'

Visit their website for more information: www.osteopathy.org.

A CHIROPRACTOR

Chiropractors are best known for treating back and neck pain. The British Chiropractor Association defines the profession as 'specialising in the diagnosis, treatment and overall management of conditions that are due to problems with the joints, ligaments, tendons and nerves, especially related to the spine. Chiropractic treatment mainly involves safe, often gentle, specific spinal manipulation to free joints in the spine or other areas of the body that are not moving properly. Apart from manipulation, chiropractors may use a variety of techniques including ice, heat, ultrasound, exercise and acupuncture as well as advice about posture and lifestyle.'

For more information visit www.chiropractic-uk.co.uk.

PREVENTING ILLNESS

If you are training hard, particularly for a marathon, you might find your body becomes run-down, leading to coughs and colds, particularly in the winter months.

Boost your immune system by having plenty of fruit and vegetables in your diet and getting lots of sleep as that's when your body repairs itself. When I was marathon training, I'd go to bed twice a week at 8.30pm since it was the only way my body could cope as I didn't have time to take a nap in the afternoon. It made me realise how important sleep is and I noticed the difference in how I looked and felt on nights when I didn't get as many hours sleep. I'm sure the extra sleep made all the difference as without it, my body would have broken down.

If you are feeling ill then it's best to back off from hard training and stick to doing no running or just short, easy runs that don't significantly raise your heart rate. Again, this is the time to listen to your body. If you are feeling low on energy and it's a real effort to run at an easy pace, then your body is telling you that you need to rest.

If you have a cold, a virus or infection then always rest until you're recovered or you could delay your recovery or make yourself worse. It's better to take a couple of days off to recuperate rather than continuing to train and then deteriorating, meaning you then have to take weeks off running.

Once you are over the worst stages of a cold, and you no longer have swollen glands and a sore throat, but are just a little bunged up, you could try doing some short, easy runs. These might help clear your head and make you feel less congested.

Never push yourself to run or race hard if you are suffering or recovering from illness. It's hard to pull out of a race you have been targeting if you are struck by illness in the days before, but in the long run it may be much better for you to do so. See if you can defer your place and focus on rest and recovery instead.

The good news is exercise can enhance your immune system so if you run regularly, you are less likely to get ill and should recover more quickly than sedentary people – as long as you are not over-training and take it easy for a few days if you do feel unwell.

If you are unsure about exercising when feeling under the weather or when taking antibiotics then always seek the opinion of your doctor.

REST & RECOVERY

Once you've got the running bug, being told you can't run for a number of days, weeks or months because of an injury or illness can seem like the end of the world. If it means missing a race you were targeting then it can be even more disappointing. However, there will always be other races you can do.

Remember it's important to rest and recover so you can come back healthier and stronger. All of the world's best athletes have had to take time off with injury at some point in their careers but get back to winning form after proper recuperation.

Don't panic about losing your fitness overnight as this won't happen from a few days' rest. A study at the University of Texas found that aerobic fitness will decrease after 12 days of inactivity[1]. Then beyond 12 days, the decrease in fitness levelled off for those who had been training for a period of time before their injury. A separate study found those who were fit before their lay-off also regained fitness faster when they were allowed to train again than those who had always been sedentary.

So the message is – don't worry when you're injured that you'll be back to 'square one' when you start training again. You will have lost some fitness, but it will be easier to regain it than it was the very first time you took up running.

If you do have to abandon running for a period of time to allow a muscle to recover or bones to repair, you may be able to do other lower-impact activities to keep your fitness up such as swimming, cycling or aqua-jogging (running in the water with a float around your waist to keep you upright).

10 TOP HEALTH TIPS

1 Eat lots of fruit and veg

2 Get plenty of sleep – at least 8 hours a night

3 Incorporate regular days off running into your training plan

4 Get regular sports massage and use a foam roller

5 Stretch

6 Dress appropriately for the weather – cool clothing, a hat and sunscreen if it's hot, thermals and waterproofs if it's cold and wet

7 Listen to your body – don't run through sharp pain or when you're feeling unwell

8 Run on a variety of surfaces (not always on concrete roads)

9 Increase mileage gradually – no more than 10 per cent extra mileage per week

10 Run in the right shoes for your running gait – visit a specialist running shop for advice if you're unsure about this

TREATING INJURY

The health benefits far outweigh the negatives, but due to the repetitive nature of running, there is a number of common injuries that may afflict most runners at one time or another. But the good news is, if treated in the correct way, they won't prevent you from training for long.

The following advice has been approved by top physiotherapist Mark Buckingham who, along with his colleagues, treats recreational runners through to Olympians at their practice in Northampton (www.wpbphysio.co.uk). If you have an injury you are unsure how to treat, you should always seek the opinion of an expert like Mark who will be able to examine you, analyse your running style and advise you on how to get back running safely again.

PULLED ACHILLES TENDON

Injury: The Achilles is a large tendon behind the heel that connects muscles in the lower leg to the heel. Sometimes it can become inflamed or, if overstretched, overloaded, sprained or torn.

Prevention: Wear the right running shoes. Ensure the shoe fits adequately so it doesn't rub at your heel and aggravate your Achilles.

Stretch your calf muscles regularly and always warm up with a gentle jog before increasing your running pace.

Mark adds: 'Poor running style with weakness in the foot and hip leads to overloading of the Achilles tendon. If in doubt seek a physio to assess you fully.'

Treatment: If you suffer from an Achilles injury, follow the RICE procedure as explained earlier in the chapter (pages 76–77). Depending on the severity of the injury, you should be able to run again after two to six weeks of rest. You can reduce this time by strengthening your Achilles through calf raises. Stand with your feet together and gently lift up your heels so you are standing on your toes. Repeat this 15 times a day. Aim to increase to 3 x 25 lifts a day.

As it gets stronger, you can progress to doing this on a step – stand on one leg (the injured one), lift on to your toes with your heel rising and falling over the edge of the step and repeat 3 x 25 times a day.

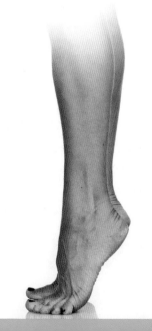

TWISTED ANKLE

Injury: Rolling on to the outside of your ankle is one of the most common running injuries and can result in varying degrees of damage.

In most cases, you may experience pain briefly, but then find it is fine to carrying on running. In other cases, it may require a few days' rest. At worst, if the ankle has been sprained and the surrounding ligaments torn with bruising and swelling, it could take up to eight weeks rest to recover.

Prevention: Watch your footing when running and be alert for potential hazards such as potholes or uneven pavements. Avoid running across particularly uneven surfaces such as football pitches with rucks, or stony paths.

Improve your lower-leg strength, posture and balance by regularly doing core stability exercises (such as 'the plank' explained on page 56) and balancing on one leg (for example, a simple way to do this without taking time out of your day is by putting your socks on without sitting down or balancing on one leg while brushing your teeth).

Treatment: The RICE principle is fundamental here as the ice, elevation and compression will reduce swelling in the ankle.

If your ankle is swollen, do not attempt to run on it until the swelling has gone down and try to avoid walking and putting weight on it as much as possible. When you can put weight on it again without intense pain, balancing exercises will help strengthen your ankle. For example, try standing on just the injured foot for 30 seconds, then try it again with your eyes closed (it will be harder to balance

this way as you can't use your sight to help stabilise your position).

You can also strengthen the ankle by doing exercises with an exercise band (aka Thera-band) – which is like a giant elastic band – that will provide resistance to your movements. Sit on the floor with your legs outstretched in front of you facing a bed or table. Wrap one end of the exercise band around a secure table leg or the bedpost, and the other around your foot. Move your toes towards you and back again, against the resistance of the band, keeping your heel in the same position, repeat 10–15 times for 3 sets. Then sit sideways to the band and turn your foot in 3 x 15 times, and then turn the other way and turn your foot out against the band, 3 x 15 times.

Listen to your body when resuming running. On a gentle strain, you should be able to run again after a few days' rest, although your ankle may still feel a bit achy. Return to full training gradually and back off if you feel any sharp pain in your ankle.

RUNNER'S KNEE

Injury: Pain above and around the knee is a common problem for runners. It often occurs as a result of muscles and fibrous tissue on the outside of the leg getting tighter and pulling the kneecap outwards from its central position.

Prevention: Run in the correct shoes for your gait to control the way your foot falls when landing.

Stretch your quads, hamstrings and IT band after every run as, if they are tight, they can pull on your kneecap.

Do exercises to specifically strengthen your quads such as squats.

Treatment: Many knee injuries are caused by a tight IT band. The best way to loosen your IT band is to see a professional sports masseur. You can also give your IT band a DIY massage by lying on a foam roller or tennis ball on the floor, sideways on, and slowly pulling your leg up it (see pictures of me demonstrating this on page 74).

PLANTAR FASCIITIS

Injury: The plantar fascia is connective tissue in the sole of the foot. It can become inflamed through overuse causing pain in the heel and arch of the foot.

Prevention: Wearing the correct shoes for your running style is important for prevention of this problem. Stretch your calf muscles regularly. As this is an overuse injury it can often occur if you have increased your training, so always up your mileage gradually.

Treatment: Roll your foot over a tennis or golf ball with your weight pressing down through the foot to give yourself a self-massage every day.

If you have a persistent problem with plantar fasciitis, see a specialist running physio. They can check your running action and identify any weakness and tightness that will lead to the plantar fascia being overloaded. 'Typically this is in the foot-stabilising muscles and the hip-stabilising muscles,' Mark says. A physio may recommend you wear orthotics in your running shoes to combat this. These are individually designed to your footfall and will correctly align and support your feet.

Having a tight plantar fascia often means you also have a tight Achilles tendon, so do the strengthening exercises for this injury.

An additional stretch involves lying on the floor with your leg straight out in front of you. Wrap a towel around your foot, then pull it taut so your toes are being pulled towards your body. Hold for 30 seconds.

PIRIFORMIS SYNDROME

Injury: The piriformis is a muscle that runs diagonally across your buttocks from the pelvis to hip. It is over the sciatic nerve so when it becomes tight it can push on the nerve, causing a sharp pain.

Prevention: The condition often afflicts people with weak glutes, quads and hamstrings so strengthen these by doing regular squat exercises.

Mark adds: 'The most common cause of persistent tightness in runners is a dysfunction in the sacro-iliac joint. This is one of two joints at the back of the pelvis. It can become stuck due to the impact of running. If the tightness has not resolved with two weeks of stretching and foam rolling (see page 75) then see a physio.'

Treatment: Trigger point massage is one of the best ways to release tension. See a professional sports masseur for treatment. You can also release the tension with a DIY home massage by sitting on a tennis or golf ball. The glute stretch described in the previous pages will help stretch the muscle.

SHIN SPLINTS

Injury: Shin splints refers to pain in the lower leg, usually at the front around the shin bone. The muscles in this area can become inflamed through overuse or because the calf muscles are too tight.

Prevention: Increase your training gradually and listen to your body. If your shins are sore it could be because you have been running too much so take a couple of days' rest or run for less time. Stretch your calf muscles regularly and always run in well-cushioned shoes.

Treatment: A sports massage will help relieve the muscles and ice will reduce inflammation. Depending on the severity of the shin splints, you should be able to keep running but reduce the time/distance. Try to run on softer surfaces such as grass rather than on the road.

A simple exercise you can do to strengthen the muscles around your shin is to sit down with your legs stretched out in front of you and then move your toes and forefeet towards your shins, repeating 10–15 times. To increase this stretch, you can also use an exercise band. In the same position as above, wrap the band around your foot and pull it taut so you are then moving your toes against the resistance from the band. Do this for 3 x 15 sets each day.

If there is no improvement and the pain in the shin increases, is being felt at rest or at night, then suspect a stress fracture (see page 85) and seek professional help.

STRESS FRACTURES

Injury: As the name suggests, a stress fracture occurs because a bone is under too much stress and fractures. The impact of running can cause fractures in people who have run for many years or suddenly take up a high-mileage schedule. Most commonly, runners suffer from stress fractures in their shins and feet, but they can also occur in the hips and back.

Prevention: Always run in well-cushioned shoes and don't just run on hard surfaces. Suffering from shin splints can often be the first sign of a stress fracture developing so take the precautions as outlined on page 84. They can occur in people with low bone density so a diet rich in calcium (found in milk and yoghurt) and vitamin D (found in oily fish and eggs) is recommended. You can also get vitamin D from exposure to sunlight.

Treatment: In extreme cases, you may need an operation or for the bone to be put in a cast, but generally rest, rest and more rest is enough to allow the bone to heal. When you return to running, usually after six to eight weeks' rest, initially only run on grass and try not to do too much too soon. Take three weeks to build up to 30 minutes' jogging. If this is pain-free then build from there.

RUNNING AS YOU AGE

As we get older, our muscle mass decreases and our metabolism slows down. We can lose flexibility and bones can become weaker. But these are not reasons to stop (or fail to start) exercising. In fact, numerous studies have found that regular training helps people stay mentally and physically younger for longer.

Exercise is particularly important to bone health as we age. As bones become less dense there is a greater of risk of the condition osteoporosis developing, which is when the bones become weaker, fragile and are more likely to fracture. As a result, a fall could lead to a serious injury such as a broken hip. Post-menopausal women are particularly at risk because they lose more bone mass annually due to the decline of the hormone oestrogen, which protects bones from calcium-loss (see Chapter 5). Professor Tim Skerry, who has researched how bones respond to exercise at the School of Medicine at the University of Sheffield, said running and weight training can counter this:

'**Running increases stamina and has important cardiovascular benefits. It also improves co-ordination and balance, so that falls are less likely, which will reduce the incidence of injuries. To have direct benefits on bone though, exercise needs to be more vigorous, even if only briefly. A few minutes of running vigorously thre e times per week is the sort of exercise that we believe can strengthen the skeleton and reduce the impact of ageing** upon it. **Strength training exercises also generally improve bone mass and architecture.**'

The benefits of exercise covered in the Why Run? chapter earlier in the book all apply to older people. If you are fit and healthy thanks to exercise, you are less likely to develop illnesses such as heart disease as you age. Regular exercise will also help you stay trim as your metabolism slows, counter-acting the dreaded 'middle-age spread' and improving mood and confidence levels.

Some people may think they are too old to take up running but it's never too late to start. A study carried out by researchers at the University of Navarra, Spain, in 2013 found exercising twice a week can help people remain stronger and more flexible well into their nineties[3]. They studied a group of people aged 91–96, who, after three months of regular exercise, had increased flexibility and muscle mass, making them stronger, more mobile and happier. So push those barriers and don't let people tell you that you can't do something because of your age. Just the other day, I met a 70-year-old man on a 10-mile run – if he can do it, so can you!

When I ran the London Marathon in 2012, a veteran athlete in his sixties, Dave Cartwright, was ahead of me the whole way and also finished in 2 hours 54 minutes (I later learnt this wasn't even his PB as he had run much faster in previous years). People like him – and Haile Gebrselassie, who is in his forties and still beating elite athletes much younger than him – show you can still run fast times as you get older.

Age is just a number so becoming a pensioner is no reason to quit training and racing. In the 2014 London Marathon, there were 204 runners aged over 70 and 15 aged over 80. The oldest runner was Paul Freedman, who ran aged 89. Meanwhile, in the elite women's field, Emma Stepo was vying for Commonwealth Games selection at the age of 44. I was also told on Twitter about an amazing woman called Eileen Quinton, who is an active member of Horsham Joggers running club at the age of 84. She regularly trains and races for the club, leaving younger runners in her wake. What an inspiration; I want to keep running as long as I can – I'd love to still be running when I'm in my eighties!

If you do take up running later in life, the same rules apply to avoid injury, including not doing too much too soon and not training through pain.

As Tim mentioned, don't be afraid to do weight training as you get older either. It's a great way to keep your bones strong and your body fighting fit into your seventies and beyond. See the cross-training section earlier in the book for strength and conditioning exercises (pages 50–57). Start off with lighter weights and build up as you get stronger.

I had to present Haile Gebrselassie with his winning trophy, such a lovely man, my hero!

HOW JACK HAS KEPT RUNNING FASTER THAN PEOPLE HALF HIS AGE INTO HIS SIXTIES

JACK BROOKS, from Hertfordshire, took up running when he was 39 and went on to achieve a marathon time of 3 hours and 12 minutes. Now in his sixties, Jack continues to race marathons around the world…

'I was inspired to start running after watching friends complete a half marathon. I started training and took part in the Lincoln Half Marathon, finishing in 2 hours and 4 minutes. I was towards the back of the field, but I couldn't believe how much support I received from fellow runners, let alone those who had turned out on a Sunday morning just to cheer us on.

'From then on I was hooked. I knew there was scope for improving my times with further training, which motivated me to keep going. I entered more races and gradually got fitter and faster.

'Ever since I've started running, I've felt much more energetic, alive and alert. Running has become an integral part of my life and I have sought to do races of various distances around the world. So apart from the obvious benefit of enabling me to keep fit, running has been responsible for me travelling extensively and making numerous good friends across the globe.

'Now I'm in my sixties, I have no intention of giving up. I still like to be competitive within my age group, but these days I tend to start towards the back of the field as it takes me longer to get up to speed and I don't like to impede faster runners.

'Thanks to running, I seem to be more active and busy than most of my non-running friends of a similar age and I'm certainly fitter than them. I'm told that I look younger than my years (although my grey hair is a bit of a giveaway!).

'My advice to anyone taking up running would be to start gradually and don't be too impatient to get fit as it takes time to build up speed and stamina. I'd also recommend joining a running club. The beauty of running is that all age groups get along so well together. You don't run with those your age but those your pace, so it's an opportunity to make friends with a variety of people. I truly love the sport and I am grateful every time I am able to go for a run.'

4: **FOOD FOR FUEL**

MY DIET

I've never been a calorie counter, but I've always tried to be a healthy eater. After taking my marathon training more seriously, I started thinking a lot more about what I was putting into my body.

As a runner, it's important to eat well and make the right food choices so you are gaining food for energy rather than comfort eating. Just imagine your body is a fine machine and you need to treat it well and fill it with the right fuel. Being more conscious about my diet has definitely helped me train and race better.

I have always been slim and when I was younger I ate what I wanted as I knew I would burn it off as I was doing enough exercise. But I was having too much refined sugar. Then when I first took up marathon training, I would just eat whatever was handy before going for a run. When I targeted a sub-three marathon, I knew I had to be more sensible about what I was eating and be more organised with the supermarket shopping so the right foods were in the house for me to eat before and after a run.

I cut right back on sugar and I noticed a real difference in how I felt and how my skin looked. In the past when I was on the go, I'd often reach for a sugary snack for an energy boost, but now I'll have fruit, nuts or seeds instead. If you are the same and frequently end up having junk food because it's more convenient when you're at work or out and about, plan ahead by packing some nuts and seeds in your handbag or boil some eggs in the morning and take them to work with you in a Tupperware box so you can snack on them later. Fish straight from the can, such as mackerel in tomato sauce or tuna in sunflower oil, is also a great protein snack when you are on the go. You don't need to drain it – just remember to get it with a pull-off top so you don't need to carry a tin opener!

Beware of some snacks such as cereal bars and yoghurts, which market themselves as healthy

because they are low fat – they could still be high in sugar. Check the nutritional information on the label and avoid those that are high in sugar (more than 22.5g of total sugars per 100g – low sugar options will have 5g or less of total sugars per 100g). Instead of having a nut bar that might contain added sugar and sweeteners, go for a bag of plain nuts instead. Or choose plain Greek or natural unsweetened yoghurt over sweetened fruit-flavoured varieties.

However, when I'm exercising regularly to burn calories I do still let myself indulge occasionally in treats like cakes and biscuits. I don't think it's good to deny yourself constantly as then you will only get cravings and overindulge. I read in Olympic marathon runner Richard Nerurkar's book *Marathon Running* that he regularly ate cake when he was marathon training – so if it's fine for him, that's good enough for me! I also love dark chocolate and I don't feel guilty about having the odd square as it's high in antioxidants and polyphenols ,which are said to prevent some diseases. It's another snack of champions: Paula Radcliffe told me she eats it regularly and has some before races.

Also, while I cut back on sugar on an everyday basis, the week before a marathon I will increase my intake by having extra strawberry jam on toast, sipping energy drinks and even snacking on Mars Bars. This means I'll have extra energy on race day, but I wouldn't eat like this if I wasn't about to run a marathon as I wouldn't burn it all off again!

WHEN AND WHAT TO EAT

It's important to start the day right with a good breakfast – especially if you then have a mid-morning training session or race. I'll often have porridge made with half rice-, oat- or soya milk and half water. You can add some honey and fresh fruit such as blueberries or strawberries to give some extra flavour and fuel.

As an alternative to porridge I'll sometimes have plain Greek yoghurt sprinkled with fruit and seeds. I also love muesli. I frequently buy Familia Swiss Muesli (and their baby version for Anya) and then add extra chia seeds, fresh fruit, chopped hazelnuts or desiccated coconut. Adding ingredients like this is a great way to customise your breakfast just how you like it and make a box go further. Breakfast choices like these should be eaten a couple of hours before training or racing to prevent a stitch or you feeling nauseous because it hasn't been fully digested.

Try to avoid doing a long run, hard session or race on an empty stomach or you could become energy-depleted. If you don't have time to digest the foods above at least 2 hours before running, then have a snack like toast or a bagel instead, which can be digested more quickly, an hour to half an hour before a run. If it's just a short, easy run you intend to do first thing in the morning, then many people find they can do this on an empty stomach with just a glass of water beforehand. If you do run before having any breakfast, make sure you refuel quickly on your return with foods like those mentioned above, or scrambled or boiled eggs or peanut butter on toast.

For lunch, I'll often have salad or a protein-packed sandwich such as avocado and mackerel on wholemeal bread, avocado with beetroot or tomato (also on wholemeal bread) or scrambled eggs with spinach on wholemeal toast.

As you can see, I eat a lot of avocado as it's full of vitamins. It's great for your skin too, so much so that many people use it as a face mask. Some people avoid avocado and nuts because they are high in fat but they're good fats – monounsaturated and polyunsaturated – which are recommended as part of a healthy diet. These types of fat can lower cholesterol and cut heart disease. Saturated and trans-fats need to be limited – they can be found in butter, whole milk, cakes and red meat.

I also eat a lot of fish like mackerel, sardines and salmon as they are full of protein and omega-3 oils which helps my recovery from a run and is said to boost brain power. They make a great snack on their own from the can or you can add fish to sandwiches, salads and pasta.

If you are running in the afternoon, have lunch a couple of hours before so it's fully digested. If you won't be able to run till later in the evening, then after lunch have a snack in the afternoon to keep you going, such as a banana, carrot sticks dipped in hummus or rice cakes.

For evening meals (which I'll always eat after running), I love using my slow cooker to make healthy but hearty stews by mixing up ingredients such as lentils, potatoes, chickpeas and various vegetables. I'll also regularly have meals such as salmon with rice and vegetables.

A TYPICAL DAY'S FOOD WHEN I AM MARATHON TRAINING

BREAKFAST	MID-MORNING SNACK	LUNCH	AFTERNOON SNACK	DINNER
Porridge or Greek yogurt with honey and fresh fruit	After a run: Big glass of milk and oat biscuits or nuts	Mackerel, eggs or avocado on wholemeal bread with salad	Nuts, fruit, occasionally a square of dark chocolate	After a run: Salmon fillet with broccoli, peas, spinach and potatoes. After a long Sunday run (of 15 miles or more), hard session or race, I'll have a recovery drink made with whey protein powder

DON'T DITCH CARBS

One of the things I love about running regularly is that I can stay in shape without having to stick to a strict diet that forbids the eating of certain food groups. In my modelling days, the girls who were on no-carb, or no-fat diets always seemed miserable. I was much happier having a decent meal and then going to the gym to stay trim.

I also think it's alarming when I hear people say they've eaten something unhealthy and as a result, 'won't eat for the rest of the day'. When I was marathon training, I wouldn't have been able to do all the runs I had planned if I didn't eat regularly. I had to keep snacking on healthy foods to keep myself energised and replenished.

Whether you are exercising or not, medical experts state it's better to follow a balanced diet including all the food groups rather than cutting any out or starving yourself. Dietitian Nichola Whitehead, who shares delicious, healthy recipes via her website www.nicsnutrition.com and Twitter account @nicnutrition, told me: 'Diets that cut out whole food groups may lead to nutritional deficiencies and I wouldn't recommend it. A balanced diet is essential for good health.'

Nichola believes the best way to ensure a healthy, balanced diet is 'to fill a third of your plate at meal times with low-GI (glycaemic index – see box on page 97) foods or wholegrain carbs (for example oats, wholemeal pasta, basmati rice, sweet potato or quinoa), a third with vegetables, fruit or salad and a third with lean protein, such as fish, chicken, eggs or lentils.'

On many weight-loss plans carbohydrates are seen as the enemy and are to be avoided at all costs. But runners need to consume ample carbs in order to train and race well. Carbohydrates are the body's main source of energy. Once consumed, they are broken down into sugars – glucose, fructose and galactose – by the digestive system. These sugars are then circulated around the body to power the muscles and vital organs such as the heart and brain.

Carbs have been given a bad name because any glucose not needed right away is stored in the muscles and the liver in the form of glycogen. Once these stores are full, if they are not used, they are then stored as fat. But if you are exercising regularly you will use these stores.

The more you exercise, the more you will need carbs to fuel your workout so you shouldn't cut them out if you're a runner, even if your reason for running is weight loss. If you do try to exercise without sufficient glucose and glycogen in your body, your performance will suffer and your body will then burn protein and muscle for energy instead. This will impair your body's recovery from exercise and damage your long-term health. So if you want to adequately fuel your run so you can perform at your best, eat plenty of carbs.

Not all carbs are created equal, so which you choose to eat is also important as they come in different forms – simple and complex. Simple carbs include table sugar and white bread. They are digested and converted into energy more quickly (because they have a high GI as explained in the box on page 97). Complex carbs include wholemeal bread, some vegetables and oats.

On a daily basis, it's better to have more complex carbs. They have a lower GI so it takes longer for your body to digest and convert them into energy. As a result, you will feel satisfied for longer. But simple carbs have their uses for runners – if you are low on energy before a training run then a quick snack of simple carbs, e.g. a slice of toast or rice cakes, can give you a boost so you feel able to do it. On a long run or marathon race they are also important as taking them in the form of energy drinks and gels will help you keep going (note you don't need to take on simple carbs during exercise unless you are covering a long distance and running for more than 2 hours).

Remember, to boost your intake of carbs you don't have to just stick to bread, potatoes and pasta. You can also have beans, such as lentils and chickpeas; nuts and seeds; rye breads; sweet potato and a vast array of vegetables. So eating carbs doesn't have to be boring or avoided!

96

CARB-LOADING

You may have heard of runners 'carb-loading' (or 'carbo-loading') before a marathon. This involves taking on extra carbs in the week before the race so your body has more glycogen stores. It is these glycogen stores that your body will rely on to get you through a long-distance race. If you don't have adequate stores, you will run out of energy, start to feel terrible and fail to keep going at your intended pace – this is known as 'hitting the wall'.

Anyone who has 'hit the wall' will know it's not a pleasant experience – it can cost you a PB and rob your race of any enjoyment. So to avoid this happening, you need to top up your glycogen stores by eating more carbs, not just the night before the race but in the preceding days too. As well as having carb-heavy meals, you should also

snack regularly on carbs such as rice cakes and bananas too.

If you are doing a marathon abroad, this may mean you have to plan your nutrition carefully. Pack plenty of carbohydrate snacks such as bagels and oat bars so you can keep snacking as you travel and aren't at the mercy of what is on offer at service stations or on a flight.

The night before the race, have a meal containing plenty of carbs, such as pasta and vegetables, and then have a carb-filling breakfast such as porridge with honey or jam.

Again, if you are racing away from home and can't prepare a meal yourself, research restaurants in the area where you are staying and check their menus in advance to ensure they have something suitable. If you are going to a restaurant, don't book the table too late in case service is slow. Your body needs time to digest the food before race day, plus you'll need an early night.

However, topping up your glycogen stores by carb-loading won't always give you enough energy to get you through the race if it's as long as 26.2 miles. That's why you also need to take on carbs during the race, which can be done by using energy drinks and gels.

These products can sometimes aggravate your gut and cause stomach cramps when running, so test out which work for you on training runs. Some major races are sponsored by brands who will only hand out their products to runners on the day, so if they are giving out a product that you've found doesn't agree with you, make sure you carry your preferred one on you instead. Personally I prefer energy drinks to gels as I don't like the taste and consistency of the latter. The first time I tried one it felt like eating snot so that put me off! That's why it's important to try different things and see what works for you.

However, while it's recommended to take on energy gels and drinks on a couple of your long runs to get used to them, don't take them on every long run you do in your marathon build-up. You want to get your body used to burning your glycogen stores when they're not topped up so you'll be more efficient at fuelling your run on race day. Taking on the drinks and gels on race day will then give you an extra boost and hopefully fuel you to a PB!

Your glycogen stores will only become depleted if you run for a long time – beyond 2 hours – so you don't need to worry about carb-loading if your target is a shorter race distance such as a 5k or 10k. You will have adequate glycogen stores from eating the daily recommend intake of carbs for a race of this length. Just make sure you have a meal rich in carbs the night before the race, such as a pasta dish, and have a carb-heavy breakfast such as porridge or toast with jam a couple of hours before the start.

WHAT'S THE GLYCAEMIC INDEX?

'GI' refers to the 'glycaemic index', which is a measure of how the body processes foods containing carbs and the speed at which they are broken down to be used as energy. Low-GI foods such as some fruits, beans, nuts and vegetables are broken down slowly. High-GI foods, such as white bread and bagels, white rice (with the exception of Basmati) and sweets are broken down quickly and cause a rapid increase in your blood glucose – giving you a spike in energy. So, to adequately fuel your running, go for low-GI foods to keep you going for longer (e.g. porridge at breakfast), but high-GI foods to give you an instant energy boost just before or during a run (e.g. jam on toast an hour before a run, or an energy gel/drink during a marathon).

Runners should eat plenty of low-GI foods but shouldn't cut out high-GI ones – as Nichola from nicsnutrition told me, it's about having a balanced diet, not one that completely favours certain food groups at the expense of others. She also agrees with me that if you are eating a balanced diet, you can still have treats such as cake occasionally – 'think moderation, not deprivation,' she says.

RUN FOR WEIGHT LOSS

If you have taken up running because you want to lose weight then good on you. The pounds will soon start falling off once you start training and raising your heart rate to burn calories. However, if you don't want to undo your hard work, don't constantly celebrate the fact you've been for a run by then overindulging in the wrong food. Just reward yourself once in a while and then it will taste even sweeter.

You should find that the more you run, the less you will want to eat unhealthy foods. A study by nutritionists at the University of Aberdeen in 2014[1] found people who had run hard for an hour were more likely to choose healthy options to eat afterwards rather than fatty foods. Numerous other findings have proved that exercise can suppress the appetite so you don't want to eat as much.

If you are running to lose weight, once you have gained some fitness, remember to include runs at

different paces and do some cross training to help you burn more calories. If you only do long, slow runs, you may find your weight stagnates. Fitness trainer Julia Buckley is an expert on the subject, having written a book, *The Fat Burn Revolution*. She explains:

'The problem with making steady running your only form of exercise when fat loss is your goal is that the body quite quickly adapts to the training. As you get fitter and are able to run for longer, your body, being the wonderful machine that it is, just keeps adapting to cope with the longer training sessions. Repeated sessions of long, slow running will cause the body to become more endurance-focused. It will then burn less fat during your training sessions and store excess calories as fat to fuel all the miles it has got used to expecting to run. So when it comes to burning fat through running, I've found the solution is to go harder, not longer. When I switched from long, steady exercise to short, high-intensity sessions and added more variety and strength training into my training mix, my body changed. The fat came off, my energy levels soared and I became healthier, stronger and fitter. So now,

Julia Buckley working out!

as a trainer, I recommend some running but in the form of high-intensity interval training (HIIT – as described in Chapter 2 with example interval sessions from Liz Yelling).

'One reason that HIIT training is super-effective is because of the 'afterburn' effect. Your metabolic rate goes through the roof during the exercise and stays elevated even after you finish training while your body adapts and recovers. This will cause you to burn more fat for 24–48 hours after exercising, depending on how intense the training was. Of course, you also get the health and fitness improvements that come as a result of working your heart, lungs and muscles harder.

'So remember, if your reason for running is to lose weight, add some variety to your training with speed work and cross training. Then you should find not only will you become slimmer, but fitter and faster too.'

Also, beware of weight gain in the weeks after you have run a marathon. It's good to reward yourself after the race (you've earned it) but don't carry on eating the way you did when you were marathon training as you won't be running the miles to burn off the extra calories. When I was training 90 miles a week, I was constantly eating because I needed the fuel, but after the race I went back to having smaller portions and fewer snacks.

I have enjoyed taking part in the Jane Tomlinson Leeds 10k, usually the race attracts around 5000 runners

HOW RUNNING HELPED ABI CHANGE HER LIFE AND LOSE 14 ST

ABI WRIGHT from Rugby took up running to lose weight but got so much more out of it than just a slimmer figure...

'Growing up I always struggled with my weight as I had no self-control when it came to food. On a daily basis, I'd have chocolate, crisps and takeaways. By my thirties, I was 25st 7lb, a dress size 32–34.

'It was becoming an aunty to my niece, Freya, and nephews, Finn and Faron, that gave me the incentive to lose weight. I could barely walk, let alone run after them at the playground, because of my size.

'I changed my eating habits, swapping my unhealthy diet for one rich in fruit and vegetables. Instead of having slices of white toast at breakfast, I'd have muesli with fresh fruit. Lunch would be a chicken salad and I snacked on fruit instead of chocolate and crisps. For dinner, I stopped eating takeaways and ready meals and had healthy dishes such as fish with vegetables. I stopped drinking fizzy drinks, having water instead.

'I wanted to get fit so I joined a gym and plucked up the courage to try running. Just taking those first running steps was an accomplishment; it was such an unknown feeling, like someone trying skiing for the first time. At first I struggled to run a mile, but I kept pushing myself and soon I was able to run for 15 minutes without stopping.

'Three months after I started running, I entered my first 5k. Completing it gave me a massive confidence boost and I loved the challenge and race atmosphere. I wanted to keep pushing myself so I went onto to do a 5-mile race, then a 10k and a half marathon.

'I had lost 14st and was finally the active aunty I had dreamed of being. Even little things like putting my socks on and tying my shoelaces was easier.

'Finishing a half marathon gave me such a high that I decided to push myself again by running the London Marathon (see how Abi got on in Chapter 6).

'I hope my story shows you don't need to have surgery to lose weight. It's healthy food and exercise that has changed my life.'

Follow Abi on Twitter @abiwrightonit.

Then: Abi weighed 25st before she took up running
Now: Abi has lost 14st

THE IMPORTANCE OF PROTEIN

While carbs are important before and during exercise, it's equally important to include protein in your diet in order to fulfil your running potential.

Our bodies need protein to make and repair tissues and cells, to fight illness and as a source of energy. Runners need extra protein to help repair muscle fibres that have been damaged by exercise. If you take on protein within an hour of hard exercise, your body will repair and recover faster. Nichola from nicsnutrition.com explains:

'Protein is an important building block in the body, and if you're working out then your protein needs will be increased. This is because exercise increases protein turnover, i.e. the rate at which your body breaks down protein (catabolism) and rebuilds it (synthesis). Protein requirements range from 0.8–2g/kg of body weight a day, with the higher amounts applying to those who are strength

training and trying to gain muscle mass. You should aim to take on board at least 20g of protein after a workout, which is the equivalent of around: 75g chicken breast/beef; half a tin of tuna/salmon; 100g turkey; 150g cottage cheese; a pint of milk; three eggs or a protein bar or shake. Failure to meet your daily protein needs could result in protein (muscle) loss, even if you are working out. In addition, protein increases satiety (keeping you fuller for longer) and contributes to a healthy immunity system – an inadequate protein intake can lead to the depletion of immune cells and the inability of the body to make antibodies (which fight infection).'

Eggs, fish, chicken and milk are all great sources of protein and can easily be eaten any time of the day. Have an omelette for breakfast or lunch and fish or chicken in salad or with pasta for a main meal. If you don't eat meat or dairy, other good sources of protein are pulses and beans such as lentils, chickpeas and kidney beans, which you can have in soups, stews, salads or sandwiches. When I was marathon training, I made sure I ate more protein than usual – lots of eggs and tins of mackerel and tuna. I felt this really helped with my recovery and as a result, my body was able to

Chocolate milk – a great post-run refuel

withstand the high mileage.

If you are at a race or have travelled away from home to do a session with your running club, having some protein soon afterwards can be difficult. That's why protein shakes are useful as they are convenient to take along to a training session or race so you can quickly drink them afterwards. They are usually made from whey. Whey is a protein found in milk that can be separated from the liquid during the production of cheese. Sports brands use whey in a powdered form so it can be mixed with water to create a drink high in protein. I love Solgar Whey To Go powder, which can be mixed with water or milk so it just tastes like a milkshake – the chocolate one is delicious. I wouldn't have one every day, just after hard sessions, races and long runs.

Some protein recovery drinks have been developed, which you can have before you go to bed. A 2012 study by the Department of Human Movement Sciences in the Netherlands[2] found that if you ingest protein after exercise and before you sleep, the protein will be effectively digested and absorbed overnight, stimulating muscle repair and making your body feel more recovered the following day. You don't need to have one every night, but if you've done a hard session in the evening or a tough race, that would be a good time to have a night recovery drink (or alternatively a glass of milk) before you go to bed to help you recover and sleep better.

If you are not training hard, such as for a marathon, then just drinking milk after a run can give you the protein you need instead of having protein shakes. Chocolate-flavoured milk has been proven to be one of the best post-run recovery drinks. Researchers in 2012 said chocolate flavoured milk is ideal as a recovery drink because it contains carbs, protein, fluid and sodium which aids in rehydration and muscle repair[4]. Stick to chocolate flavoured milk rather than milkshakes as the latter is often made using fattening ice cream.

SUPPLEMENTS

A dietary supplement is a product intended to add further nutritional value to the diet and is taken in the form of a tablet, powder or drink. People might take supplements if they feel their diet is lacking in a certain nutrient, e.g. people might take a daily vitamin C tablet if they don't eat much fruit (but it's better to have fruit if you can).

I don't eat red meat, which is rich in iron, so instead I have two sachets of Spatone, a natural iron supplement, every day. Iron is important because it helps create red blood cells, which carry oxygen around the body. If you are deficient in iron, you can feel tired and weak. Women in particular are prone to iron deficiency because of menstruation, which is why taking a supplement can be useful. Iron is best absorbed if it is taken with vitamin C such as orange juice. Caffeine can hinder absorption so you shouldn't take an iron supplement with a cup of tea or coffee.

However, consult your doctor if you are concerned about your iron levels (for example, if you constantly feel tired and low in energy even though you are eating well and getting plenty of sleep). They can give you a blood test to investigate if your iron levels are too low. Most people can get their daily iron requirements from a balanced diet. It can be found in foods such as red meat, nuts and seeds, broccoli and leafy green vegetables like kale. You shouldn't take on extra iron if you don't need to because it can cause constipation.

As I said earlier, I also use protein supplements when I'm training hard to aid my recovery. Dietitian

Nichola also recommends such products to help you re-fuel quickly and conveniently:

'Whey protein-based bars and shakes can be a convenient, low-calorie and low-volume way of helping one to achieve daily protein needs, and a bar or shake can make a super-tasty and healthy snack after a workout. Whey protein is absorbed relatively quickly and contains the branched-chain amino acid leucine, which helps to preserve lean tissue (muscle). But of course, food always comes first... protein bars/shakes should be used as a dietary supplement and not a replacement for food (studies have actually shown that milk, which contains whey naturally, is just as effective at promoting muscle growth after exercise as supplements).'

It is always best to meet your nutritional needs with real foods, but supplements can be an easy and convenient way to top up your intake, especially if you can't eat certain foods due to allergies, for religious reasons or personal taste or ethical preferences.

If you do decide to take supplements, always buy them from a reputable source and ensure they have been tested for the situation in which you

intend to use them. Sadly, Claire Squires, 30, didn't do this when she took part in the London Marathon in 2012. I was devastated to hear how she collapsed and died after running 25 miles of the race. A coroner later ruled she had died of cardiac failure caused by extreme exertion, complicated by taking the now banned drug, DMAA. Claire had innocently added a scoop of the product into her water bottle for the race thinking it would be ok since it was an ingredient in a supplement she had bought online called Jack3D. The product is a stimulant that raises the heart rate and was used by serious gym users to prolong their workout. Claire thought it would give her a boost in the final stages of the marathon and prevent her from hitting the wall. However, it was not safe to take the product during a long-distance run. The combination of a raised heart rate from running the marathon with the stimulus caused by the drug was too much for her heart to take.

We can't bring Claire back but we can learn from her story – check the ingredients of products you intend to take and be wary of companies whose promises to make you a better athlete by taking their product seem too good to be true. There is no substitute for hard work in training and following a healthy, balanced diet when it comes to improving your health and fitness – so view supplements as a means of aiding your training rather than as a miracle fitness fix.

STAYING HYDRATED

We all need water to survive as it's vital for almost every bodily function. Most people don't drink enough fluid every day, which could lead to them feeling tired and sluggish.

If you are out all day working, take a bottle of water with you from which you can sip throughout the day and remember hot drinks count towards your recommended daily fluid intake. Tea and coffee were once thought to be dehydrating because they are a diuretic (meaning that they enhance the production of urine). However, it has been disproven that they are dehydrating, but they will make you need the toilet more (so beware drinking too much before a run or race or you'll need to make frequent loo stops along the way!)

I often have a coffee in the morning and caffeine has been proven to be beneficial to runners. Caffeine is a stimulant so it can make you feel more awake and alert and numerous studies have also shown it can improve endurance.

Runners in particular need to stay refreshed because water is lost through sweat when exercising. If you don't take on enough water during or after exercise, you can become dehydrated, which can lead to light-headedness, headaches and sometimes nausea. Being dehydrated when racing can impair your performance, meaning you don't run to your full potential.

Taking on too much water while exercising can also be detrimental – and in rare extreme cases fatal – causing a condition known as hyponatraemia. This is when too much water has been consumed so it flushes too much salt from the body and can cause the brain to swell.

With this in mind, it's vital to strike a balance of how much water you take on, particularly in a long run like the marathon. Most big city races have frequent water stations, but you don't need to guzzle a whole bottle at each station. Instead, drink little but often from early on in the race – and crucially don't wait until you are thirsty to start drinking as by then you'll already be suffering from the symptoms of dehydration.

How much water you need to drink on a daily basis depends on your body weight and height – as well as how active you are. The shade of your urine is the best indicator of how hydrated you are – it should be a clear colour. The darker it is, the more dehydrated you are.

When running, remember how much you need to drink will be dependent on how much you sweat. So on hotter days you will need to drink more as you will be sweating more. You will also need to drink more if you are working yourself hard in a race, interval session or long run or in the gym, where you are likely to get hotter.

To ensure you can stay hydrated on a long training run, try wearing a belt around your waist that can hold a water bottle. You can also get bottles which are shaped to easily be held in your hand. Or, if you don't want to carry a bottle during a training run, pick a route during which you will pass a certain point more than once and hide your water bottle there so you can make stops to drink.

It's better – and cheaper – to drink plain water before and during exercise on a daily basis. Avoid drinking energy and fizzy drinks regularly as they are high in sugar – stick to having energy drinks on long runs and endurance races when you can reap the benefits of the sugar intake to boost your performance. If you are doing a training run of less than an hour, or a race shorter than a half marathon, you shouldn't need to take on an energy drink – water should be sufficient. When I'm racing, I often only take on energy drinks in a marathon. The first few times at London I drank the Lucozade that was provided, but when I ran sub-three, I carried my own SIS carbohydrate drink, which is powder mixed with water. In races shorter than the marathon and training runs, I'll stick to water.

After exercising, drinking milk will help rehydrate you and the added protein will help your body recover faster. Try a protein shake as explained on pages 102–103 if you have done a hard training session or race.

ALCOHOL

I only drink alcohol on rare occasions these days and I never drank when I was in training for an important race, as I would never have been able to face running with a hangover! But being a runner doesn't mean you have to give it up completely. It's fine to have the odd tipple but if you want to take your training seriously, you should avoid drinking too much. Excess alcohol will hinder your ability to sleep, train and race well. If you've ever had a bad hangover, you'll know it's difficult to get out of bed, let alone go for a run, so you'll never be able to train hard if you're overindulging in alcohol on a regular basis. You'll never race to the best of your ability either, so if you've trained hard for a race, don't let all your efforts go to waste by getting drunk the night before. Some people find one glass of their favourite drink can calm their nerves the night before the race but if you can manage without doing this, you'll be far better off. Drinking too much could actually prevent you from having a good night's sleep. Not only is alcohol excess calories that you don't need, it's also dehydrating. So if you do have an alcoholic drink the night before a run, you'll need to drink plenty of extra water to rehydrate the day after. It's better to avoid alcohol in the lead-up to a race and then have a celebratory drink afterwards. But if you do this, remember to also have water to aid your recovery.

SOME OF MY FAVOURITE FOODS AND WHY THEY'RE GOOD FOR RUNNERS

AVOCADO

This fruit is high in 'good' fats and vitamins. It's been proven to boost heart health and will also give you glowing skin. Put it in a salad or spread it on wholemeal bread and sandwich it with chickpeas, beetroot or tomatoes.

CHIA SEEDS

These have been fuelling runners since Aztec times, when they were dissolved in water and used as an energy drink. They are high in carbs, protein and omega-3 and can stabilise blood sugar levels, giving you more energy. They are tasteless so you can add them to salad, yoghurt, porridge or smoothies or dissolve them in water for an energy drink, like the Mexican Tarahumara long-distance runners still do. I add a spoonful to muesli in the morning.

PUMPKIN SEEDS

These are high in magnesium, which is needed for strong bones and muscle function. Eat a handful as a snack during the day or sprinkle over porridge, a salad or a risotto.

NUTS

All nuts are rich in health-boosting vitamins and minerals and 'good' fats, so try to regularly eat a variety. Buy a big bag of mixed nuts (they're better for you if they're plain and not coated in salt or yoghurt) and snack on a handful each day.

OATS

These are full of fibre and carbs and are great before exercise because they provide slow-release energy. They also contain magnesium and can lower cholesterol when eaten regularly. Have porridge in the morning or snack on low-sugar oatcakes or oat bars.

MILK

Packed with calcium, milk is excellent for giving you strong bones, but it's also high in protein, making it a great recovery drink after exercise.

FRUIT

Fresh and dried fruit makes a great snack on the go or at home. All fruits are good for you thanks to their vitamin content so it's good to mix up which you have each day to gain the benefits and make the most of what's in season. Eat a banana before exercise as it contains quick energy-release carbs. Sprinkling fresh fruit such as blueberries, strawberries or raspberries on your breakfast cereal, porridge or yoghurt is a great way to start the day. Dried fruit such as raisins and dried apricots still contain fibre and nutrients but are higher in calories than fresh fruit so shouldn't be eaten as regularly. Go for dried fruits that don't contain added sugar and that aren't covered in chocolate or a sweet yoghurt coating.

BEETROOT

This vegetable has become a runner's best friend after numerous studies have shown the nitrates it contains can help improve stamina and endurance[3]. In the studies, athletes who had drunk beetroot juice used oxygen more efficiently while exercising so they could keep going for longer. Try drinking beetroot juice an hour before running or add cooked slices to salads or sandwiches. Note; pickled beetroot from a jar won't give you the same health benefits.

SPINACH

This leafy green vegetable also contains nitrates so can boost endurance in the same way as beetroot. It's also full of vitamins and is a rich source of iron. Add it to curries and stews, use it to make soup or have it with scrambled eggs or an omelette. The uncooked leaves can be added to salad.

FISH

Fish is low in fat and high in protein. Runners can gain numerous benefits from eating it regularly. After exercising, the protein will help your muscles repair. Omega-3 in fish is also good for your joints. I love fish sandwiches or it makes an ideal quick snack straight from the can. Baked or steamed fillets of salmon make a delicious evening meal with vegetables and some wholegrain rice.

CHICKPEAS

These are a great source of protein, particularly if you are vegetarian. You can use them in homemade curries or stews or make them into a hummus dip to have with carrot and celery sticks.

WHOLEMEAL BREAD

Opt for wholemeal over white bread as it contains slow-release energy and will keep you fuller for longer. Seeded loaves will also give you an added vitamin boost.

KIDNEY BEANS

High in protein and fibre, kidney beans have been proven to lower the risk of heart attack in people who consume them regularly. They are also an excellent source of iron. I love them mixed with mackerel or tuna or in a stew.

5: **JUST FOR WOMEN**

INSPIRING ROLE MODELS

It's wonderful that women's participation in running is on the up. Running is accessible to women of all ages and backgrounds and we have some amazing role models to look up to.

A number of different factors affect women when running that aren't of concern for men, from running through your period to keeping fit during and after pregnancy. That's why I've dedicated a whole chapter of the book to women.

I admire and respect elite male runners and I think they make great role models. But it's female athletes who have really inspired me over the years and helped me believe anything is possible with the right training. I remember reading about Tracey Morris in 2004, when she had the race of her life to qualify for the Athens Olympics. She was an optician working in Leeds and she smashed her PB and became an Olympian. She was 37 at the time, which shows you don't have to be young to run well. It was her time to shine and it shows what can be achieved when you put the training in.

Liz McColgan is another of my running heroines. With little support at the beginning, she became a world-class athlete and won numerous championship titles and medals, proving that with lots of hard work and determination you can succeed. She later juggled her elite running career with motherhood. She's long retired from elite competition but is still super-fit. She has five children and has coached her daughter, Eilish, to follow her Olympic dream by becoming a world-class steeplechaser. I've had the pleasure of meeting Liz

and she told me running will always be a part of her life. She said:

'The reason I run has come full circle. When I was 12, I ran because it allowed me to escape from the poverty and the tough life around me. I found through running I could solve all my worries and problems. Running then became an obsession and something I was very good at. It became about how hard I could push myself, not about medals. I needed to prove how good I was to everyone and to myself – I feel I never quite satisfied that desire. Now my running is back to escapism, anything that

Liz McColgan in 1995 at the World Championships

Paula Radcliffe breaking her own world record in the 2003 London Marathon

stresses me or worries me I can only sort out and chill out with a run. I can't imagine running not being part of my life.'

It's incredible to think that just 40 years ago women were considered 'too weak' to run long distances. It wasn't until 1972 that women were allowed to race further than 1500m in the Olympics. They weren't allowed to compete in the marathon until the Los Angeles Olympics in 1984.

While a number of plucky women had previously unofficially taken part in the marathon, it was Kathrine Switzer who brought the issue to the attention of the world's media when she entered the Boston Marathon in 1967 using her initials on the entry form. When the organisers realised she was a woman, they physically tried to remove her from the race. But Kathrine was determined to finish, doing so in 4 hours and 20 minutes. After that, she trained harder to improve her time alongside campaigning tirelessly for a woman's right to race.

It's daring women like Kathrine who we have to thank for being able to compete in long-distance races today. She once said that running makes her feel 'powerful, free and fearless' and that says it all. All women can gain that feeling from running, it doesn't have to be a marathon but could just be a run around the park.

Since being allowed to compete, a number of women – including another of my heroines, Paula Radcliffe – have gone on to prove women can be fast, strong and competitive. Paula's amazing marathon World Record of 2 hours and 15 minutes shows women can run faster than many men and that we can train and race as hard as they do. Paula told me the key to her success was:

'a lot of hard work and attention to detail by the whole team around me. They all helped me to get the very best out of myself. I also believe that because I love doing what I do and really enjoyed my racing that helped me to get more out of myself and have a longer career.'

Meanwhile, in ultra-distance running, female athletes like Lizzy Hawker win races outright leaving men to eat their dust. That's real girl power.

RUNNING & MENSTRUATION

For many runners, the arrival of their period once a month is more of an inconvenience than a problem. It should not prevent you from training thanks to the useful products on the market that help you stay active, including tampons and menstrual cups.

However, some symptoms women experience at their time of the month make it harder to train and race well – from feeling tired and sluggish to suffering from stomach cramps and water retention. Dr Juliet McGrattan explains:

'Although some studies have shown that women's athletic performance is not affected by their menstrual cycle, the majority of women report they train more effectively, feel better and run faster at different times of the month. The worst time seems to be pre-menstrual – in the week before their period – when they feel sluggish and bloated. Once the bleeding starts things usually improve rapidly and after the heavier blood loss in the first couple of days of a period it's often a great time to run.'

However, many women can suffer from crippling period pain in the form of stomach cramps, which can make getting out of bed difficult, let alone going for a run. But Juliet says a gentle run could actually alleviate the symptoms and make you feel mentally as well as physically better.

She adds that if you don't want the pain to stop you sticking to your training schedule – or if you have a race that day – you could take some painkillers. 'Use simple paracetamol rather than non-steroidal anti-inflammatories, such as

Ibuprofen, which can be harmful to your kidneys if you get dehydrated,' she advises.

For those who really suffer during their periods, Juliet says a visit to your own GP could help:

'If your important race day coincides with your period you may be able to delay your bleeding by getting a progesterone tablet from your GP. If your periods frequently interfere with your running and you don't mind using contraception, then there are methods available to regulate, lighten your bleeding or stop your periods altogether. This can be a real bonus for lots of runners.'

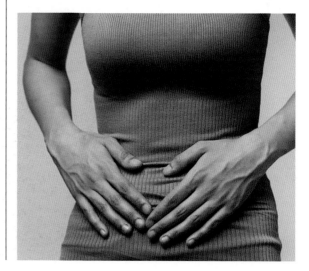

Juliet also recommends eating plenty of iron if you are someone who experiences heavy periods because you could become anaemic. Athletes and vegetarians are particularly at risk of iron deficiency. Anaemia means there are fewer red blood cells in your body and oxygen is not transported to your muscles fast enough. Training while anaemic will mean you tire easily, get short of breath and underperform.

Iron-rich foods include beef, mussels and oysters. Vegetarians can get iron from pumpkin seeds, nuts and green vegetables such as broccoli and spinach. If you are concerned about your iron

levels, you can ask your GP to give you a blood test. They may recommend you take a daily iron supplement. As I mentioned previously in the Food For Fuel chapter, as I don't eat red meat, I keep my iron levels topped by taking a natural iron supplement every day, which comes in a sachet you can drink.

When some women are training hard and doing high mileage, their periods can become irregular or cease altogether, known as amenorrhea. It is most common in female athletes with low body fat because they are not taking in enough calories to fuel their training regime. As the body doesn't have enough fuel to perform all its normal functions, it shuts down the ones that aren't vital – such as the reproductive system. This is obviously a problem for women who are trying to conceive, but amenorrhea also causes other serious health concerns.

Amenorrhea is a sign the body is under too much stress and is deficient in the nutrients it needs to be healthy. This will have a knock-on effect on your energy levels, appearance and athletic performance. Worst of all, women with amenorrhea have been found to have lower bone density. This makes them at higher risk of an injury such as a stress fracture while they are training and could ultimately lead to osteoporosis – when the bones become brittle and can break easily.

This is why it's vitally important to eat well when you are training. For those who fear weight gain, remember it's not about over-indulging. As covered in the Food For Fuel chapter, it's about making the right food choices and eating sensible portions. Eating lots of nutritious foods will fuel the exercise you are doing, help your body recover afterwards and ensure you have a happy, healthy body.

RUNNING & CONCEIVING

If you are trying for a baby and have a normal menstrual cycle then you should be able to carry on running while trying to conceive.

If however, your periods have stopped or become irregular because of hard training and you are experiencing amenorrhea as explained above, you should reduce the intensity of your training and increase your daily intake of calories. This should eventually lead to your periods resuming.

If you are desperate to have a baby but struggling to conceive, then running could be highly beneficial to you during this time. It should make you feel less stressed, prevent excess weight gain and give you a strong, fit body in which to carry a baby.

BABY ON BOARD

As I've always been fit and active, I wanted to keep running during both my pregnancies. If I had any pregnancy complications then of course I wouldn't have run. But because my pregnancies were both normal and my body was used to exercise, there was no reason why I should hang up my trainers. In fact, there's a lot to be gained from running during pregnancy for mother and baby.

However, if you have never run before, during pregnancy is not the time to start. Instead you should stick to walking or swimming to gain the benefits of exercising while pregnant.

When I told people I was still running – and it was reported in the press that I was doing 6 miles a day while 20 weeks pregnant – I did receive some criticism. People who didn't know any better said exercising when pregnant is selfish and can harm an unborn baby. But that couldn't be further from the truth. It's not like smoking or drinking alcohol while pregnant, it's doing something that's good for the health of you and your child.

I feel many people have misinformed views on exercise during pregnancy because there isn't that much information out there. That's one of the reasons why this book came about. I hope the information reassures other expectant mothers that it's fine to carry on running if they want to.

If you are a runner who chooses not to run during your pregnancy, that's also fine. It's not a time to run because you have to in order to do well in a race or because you feel under pressure to keep fit. It's a time to run because you enjoy it and it makes you feel good.

Running definitely helped me feel better physically and emotionally during my pregnancies. In the first trimester, being out in the fresh air doing some easy runs alleviated any morning sickness and revived me. I always felt like I had more energy and vitality after I ran. Throughout my pregnancies I didn't suffer from swollen ankles or a lack of energy and I'm fairly sure that's because I was keeping fit and healthy.

All the benefits of running covered in the Why Run section of the book still apply when you are pregnant. It will make you healthier and boost your confidence and mood. This is particularly important during pregnancy when you have different hormones coursing through your body, and may feel worried about impending motherhood.

I ran for about 30 to 40 minutes a day during the first seven months of both my pregnancies. This might sound like a lot to some, but before I fell pregnant with Anya, I had been marathon training doing 90 miles a week. So this was a much lower mileage than I had been doing and my body could handle it. I also ran at a much slower pace than before. So how much you run when you are pregnant should be relative to your pre-pregnancy fitness and previous training. Just ensure you decrease both the duration and intensity of all your runs – your weekly mileage should be a lot less than it was before. You shouldn't be doing any exceedingly longs runs (of more than an hour) or interval sessions during which you raise your heart rate. Instead, stick to an easy, comfortable pace at which you could have a conversation and take care not to overheat.

As long as there are no complications in the pregnancy, both the Royal College of Obstetricians and Gynaecologists (RCOG)[1] and the NHS[2] advocate moderate exercise when pregnant of around 30 minutes a day. In a statement on their website, the RCOG write: 'In most cases, exercise is safe for both mother and fetus during pregnancy and women should therefore be encouraged to initiate or continue exercise to derive the health

I found power walking a great way to keep fit when I felt too uncomfortable to continue running. Just being out in the fresh air made me feel better, happier, fitter and healthier

benefits associated with such activities.' They add that it's a fallacy that exercise increases the risk of miscarriage or damage to an unborn baby stating 'women should be advised that adverse pregnancy or neonatal outcomes are not increased for exercising women.'

They explain that exercising while pregnant have been shown to have numerous benefits for the mother's health and well-being that are both 'physical and psychological in nature'. For example, they explain: 'Many common complaints of pregnancy, including fatigue, varicosities (i.e. large and painful varicose veins) and swelling of extremities, are reduced in women who exercise. Additionally, active women experience less insomnia, stress, anxiety and depression.'

I found I slept well (until the last trimester) and felt happy throughout both my pregnancies and I'm sure that's because I was exercising.

Another benefit of exercising while pregnant is you don't gain excess body fat. I gained about a stone-and-a-half each time and both my babies were born a healthy size – Devon weighed 7lb 8oz and Anya 7lb 10oz. Many women eat too much when pregnant, believing they have to 'eat for two', but no extra calories are actually needed until the third trimester – and then it's only a further 200Kcal a day. An added bonus of exercising during pregnancy is that you will need some extra calories to replace to those you've burnt off exercising, so this means you can give into your cravings occasionally if they are for cake or chocolate!

It's advisable not to gain too much excess fat while pregnant. It's not about vanity but because obesity in pregnancy can cause a host of complications including diabetes and pre-

eclampsia. It could also mean you have to have a caesarean or have a baby with an abnormally high birth weight. Research has found that babies of overweight women are more likely to grow up to be obese themselves, so by doing gentle exercise and not over-indulging while pregnant, you will be setting up your child to have a healthier future. You could also make them cleverer. In 2013, neuroscientists in Canada found that babies of mothers who exercised while pregnant had enhanced brain development[3]. Exercising for 20 minutes three times a week made a difference.

As my baby bump grew, I spent most of my time in my running gear as the stretchy Lycra was more accommodating for my expanding waistline. As your bump grows, there is no need to worry about your baby 'bouncing' around in the womb when you are running. They are completely surrounded by fluid, which protects them from movement outside the womb.

By the time I was seven months pregnant, running was becoming less comfortable because of my size. At this time, you have to be aware that the bump will affect your balance and centre of gravity so falling or tripping over while running becomes more likely. I felt it wasn't a risk worth taking so I began power walking, swimming and going to the gym instead of running.

At 36 weeks when I was carrying Anya, I regularly lifted small hand weights. While holding the weights, I did reps of squats, lunges and bicep curls. I wanted to focus on strengthening my legs, arms and back muscles. After having Devon, I spent hours hunched over breastfeeding and changing nappies so I often got backache. Plus carrying a new baby can become tiring for your arms and

back as the baby gets bigger. So the second time around I felt I was better prepared by doing some light weightlifting work. I used to joke that I might go into labour when lifting weights in the gym!

One thing to remember if you go to the gym or exercise at home while heavily pregnant, is to avoid any moves that involve lying flat on your back as this can cause your blood pressure to drop due to the weight of the baby bump on top of you.

When you decide to stop running and exercising when pregnant is your own personal decision. Some women stop after a few months, while others carry on till the week before their due date. Physiotherapist Mark Buckingham (www.wpbphysio.co.uk), who offered his expert advice on injury prevention and recovery earlier in the book, has worked with numerous pregnant athletes. He told me:

'The typical woman who runs or plays sport will each have their own cut-off point. There is no right or wrong time to slow or stop activity. It is important to listen to your own body and not try to make yourself do what you think you ought to. I saw a lady today who said at 23 weeks running became uncomfortable, so she stopped. She could swim and walk fine, so that is what she did instead.'

Mark says it's safe to run while pregnant as long as you are not pushing yourself to run hard or covering long distances. In particular, he said women should not force themselves out of the door if they are feeling tired. He explains:

'Running tired puts greater strain on the body when it is already working hard building a baby. It uses precious energy reserves and leaves you and your immune system run down (pardon the pun). This means you are more at risk from illness.

When I was pregnant with my first child, leading the warm-up for the Race for Life at Temple Newsam, Leeds

Running tired also means you are less able to maintain good posture and form. This puts unwanted stresses on the lower back and pelvis at a time when it is most vulnerable. Clearly as the pregnancy develops the loads are greater, the posture inevitably changes and the risks are higher. You have to listen to your body and react to how it feels, not how you would like to run.'

As long as women adhere to Mark's advice, he says running while pregnant can bring many benefits including 'maintenance of cardiovascular fitness, blood-pressure control, maintenance of good circulation, feelings of well-being and enhanced abdominal, lower back and leg strength', which he says are all 'big positives as much as for getting back on your feet after birth as for during it'.

Mark points out that it's in the third trimester that women have to be extra vigilant about exercising. He explains:

'It is the third trimester when the biggest changes

occur. The end of the third trimester is when the hormone relaxin (which makes ligaments lax and stretchy to help the baby's delivery), really kick in. It is these hormones that pose the biggest risk of long-term injury for pregnant athletes. They make impact work like running more likely to have a detrimental effect on areas like the feet, and especially the pelvis. The pelvis is held together by three fibrous joints. Pregnant women have less pelvis stability towards the end of their pregnancy because relaxin acts to make the fibrous ligaments around these joints stretch during childbirth. The repeated impact on the joints from running in the third trimester can make the pelvis more likely to shift. The forward tilt of the pelvis due to the baby's weight also makes this shift more likely to happen. With this forward tilt, the lumbar spine is arched to its 'end of range' and becomes compressed and painful. Many pregnant women will be familiar with this back pain. There is much that can be done to help it but the avoidance of those activities that cause pain is the first thing to do.'

This is why it's often better to stick to low-impact activities such as walking or swimming at the end of your pregnancy rather than pounding the pavements or treadmill.

If you have been exercising earlier in your pregnancy, you can then put your feet up and rest with the knowledge it could make your labour 'easier'. Of course childbirth is never easy – in my experience it's much harder than running a marathon – but by keeping fit I felt I was better prepared to handle the stress and pain of labour. According to the RCOG, exercising while pregnant also makes the baby able to 'tolerate' labour better than babies of inactive mothers.

TIPS FOR RUNNING WITH A BUMP

Don't start running while pregnant if you haven't run before

Decrease your weekly mileage and don't do any long runs (beyond an hour)

Keep the pace slow and easy – use a GPS or heart rate monitor to help you control your pace and keep your heart rate down

Don't run through any pain or discomfort, if something hurts, stop running

Avoid running on uneven surfaces and hilly terrain

Don't run on very hot days when you could be at risk of overheating

Don't run if you're feeling exhausted

When your bump gets bigger, try running with a maternity support belt, available from shops like Mothercare. They give your bump some extra support and should ease some back pain and make running more comfortable

Don't feel obliged to run or stick to a training plan – you should be running because you enjoy it and it enhances your well-being

HOW RUNNING THROUGH PREGNANCY MADE ME FEEL MORE PREPARED FOR CHILDBIRTH

CHRISTINA SMITH, 39, has three children, Adam, Millie and Sadie, with husband Mike. She feels it's no coincidence her easiest pregnancy was the one during which she was at her fittest...

'I didn't run for that long during my first pregnancy when I was age 31. As I was working full-time, I was often too tired and too short on time. After my son, Adam, was born, I started getting back into running when he was about six months old by attending my running club's Tuesday evening sessions. I started to feel fitter and faster again, but then a few months later, when Adam was only 10 months, it suddenly became more of an effort to maintain a pace I'd previously found easy – I was pregnant again!

'This time I wasn't able to run at all as I felt ill for the entire 39 weeks. As I was so poorly, and then anaemic, I wasn't allowed to do any exercise – and I wouldn't have been capable even if I was allowed!

'Millie was born at 39 weeks, but was (and still is) a poorly child. I tried to resume running when I had recovered from the birth – but my heart wasn't in it that much so training was intermittent.

'By the time Millie was two, I was running more and started doing some 5k and cross-country races. After a particularly exhausting cross-country race, during which I didn't run as well as I'd hoped, I soon discovered the wonderful reason why – I was pregnant again.

'This time I ran until the week before my baby arrived. I felt much better throughout this pregnancy than my previous two, so I decided that I would try and run for as long as I could. Initially I thought this would mean I'd run until the six-month mark, but as I felt good I carried on.

'Despite having a five-year-old and a four-year-old to run around after, my third pregnancy was the one in which I had the most energy and felt the best. Whether that's due to running or not I don't know for sure. But I do know getting out for an easy run was invaluable for keeping my head together and just giving me some space away from the demands of two small children! And a happy, healthy mummy usually makes for a happy, healthy baby.

'As my bump grew, I used a maternity support belt while running from 28 weeks onwards. This alleviated any stress on my back and helped to support the bump. I never ran faster than a pace at which I wasn't comfortable to talk and I avoided routes that would involve going up or down hills. I also had to plot routes along which there were toilets as I needed the loo a lot!

'Taking part in my local parkrun was a great way for me to still run once a week late into my pregnancy without any worries. Should anything have happened there were plenty of people around to make sure I was OK. It was also rewarding when people who had just taken up running spoke to me after the run and said I inspired them to keep going. They said if I could do it when pregnant they had no excuse not to keep going.

'Keeping running meant I didn't put on as much weight as in my previous pregnancies, in fact most people commented that I didn't look pregnant at all until quite late on. By the time I was full-term, I had gained exactly one-and-a-half-stone and because I was fitter, I felt more prepared for childbirth.

'Sadie was born at 41 weeks. I didn't have any pain relief yet it was definitely my 'easiest' labour. Perhaps this was because it was my third so I knew what to expect, but I'm sure my fitness was a factor.

'This time around I got back into my running routine much more easily. Once Sadie was six weeks old, I would train in the evenings when my husband got home from work. Sometimes it would only be a very short run around the block, but that was still better than nothing.

'It isn't easy to fit running in with three children but we manage. Sometimes friends or family babysit so Mike and I can run together or we take the children with us to the parkrun. Now Adam is older, he sometimes joins me on his bike while I run. On other occasions I fit running in with what we're doing, so if we're going to the supermarket or taking the children swimming, I'll run there while Mike drives. The children see it as a fun game where I'm racing them to the destination.

'If I had to give any advice to other mums running while pregnant, I'd say not to fear exercising. Staying physically active is good for your health, stress levels and general birthing preparation.

'After giving birth, I've learnt to resume running when you feel mentally and physically ready – don't put a time limit on it. It took me two years after one baby and weeks after another. So listen to your body, you'll know when the time is right.

'Remember any run is better than no run, especially on those days when the baby has screamed all day and you are exhausted – even just a 5-minute jog can actually revive you.

'I continued breastfeeding when I resumed running, but I learnt to feed the baby first, wear a good sports bra (I wore two sometimes!) and refuel quickly afterwards so as not to affect my milk production.

'I think running is great for mums and children. When they see you running it gives them a positive role model and sets them up for a healthy future. Adam is already a keen runner and it teaches him and my daughters to respect their amazing bodies and to want to be healthy and eat right. It also teaches them perseverance, determination, commitment and discipline – all attributes that will aid them in other areas of their lives as they grow up.

Family fun: Chris doing a fun run with son Adam while pregnant with her daughter, Sadie

RUNNING AFTER PREGNANCY & CHILDBIRTH

Once your baby has arrived, I'm sure running will be the last thing on your mind and you'll just want to spend time with your precious newborn.

If you do start to get itchy feet about running, then be patient. You should not run at all for the first six to eight weeks after labour. If you had a caesarean, you may need to rest for a few more weeks as it will take your body longer to heal. If you are concerned about whether your body is ready, check with your doctor before you resume running.

As explained on pages 120–121, the hormone relaxin is released in pregnant women to make the body more supple and stretchy for childbirth. This hormone is still in the body for weeks after labour, which is why it's important not to run and impact your joints. Failing to do so could cause you to pull a muscle or it could do permanent damage to your pelvis and spine. Physiotherapist Mark Buckingham explains:

'I have personally seen too many athletes come to me with nasty pelvic and spine issues caused by a return to running in the first few days, let alone weeks, after birth. Some actually never return to running as the damage they cause by too much too soon can be permanent. The old wives' adage of nine months to have a baby and nine months to get over it is close to the mark.'

If you do want to get out in the fresh air in the first six to eight weeks after your pregnancy, then stick to walking instead of running. This is what I did after both of my children were born. I was so tired from the sleepless nights, I don't think I would have had the energy to run even if I had wanted to.

Another thing you should do to help your body recover from labour and become strong again is pelvic floor exercises. Your health visitor should be able to advise you on this and there is also some more information provided in the section on dealing with stress incontinence later in this chapter.

Once Anya was about two months old, I started running again about two times a week if I had time to fit it in. I just did short runs at an easy pace. On some days I felt good, on others I felt like I was jetlagged and depleted of energy because I was breastfeeding on demand and sleep deprived. I also tried to fit in exercises at home while Anya had naps during the day, such as doing the plank and press-ups. But I was a lot weaker than I had been before pregnancy. I could barely hold the plank for a few seconds and could only manage a few press-ups before needing a rest. I was a long way from the fitness I had before Anya was born, but I didn't worry about it.

Four months after Anya was born I had agreed to take part in *Women's Running* magazine's 10k in

The Kielder Marathon

Nottingham. I was looking forward to it and, in the past, knowing I had a race on the horizon would have motivated me to train harder. But I knew after having a baby is not the time to think about setting PBs, it's just time to keep your fitness ticking over.

So that's one important piece of advice I would give to new mothers who are used to keeping fit – don't get frustrated about not being as fit or as fast as you once were. Enjoy the time you have with your new baby – they grow up so fast and there will be plenty of time for you to train and race when they are older. If you try to rush back into training you are more likely to become injured. But if you are patient and sensible, you can run well again. I certainly intend to have a crack at beating my PBs in the future, but I'll wait until Anya is a bit older.

Mark says he has treated numerous athletes who have returned to their previous form – or surpassed it – after becoming mothers. He explains:

'Those athletes who have taken their time in returning to running, allowing the body to recover, have all returned to their previous level, and sometimes beyond, from club runners to internationals.

When you do have the time and energy to resume training after pregnancy, remember to build your training up gradually like you would if you were starting running for the first time, or coming back from time off due to an injury. Listen to your body and don't run through pain.

You should not feel any pressure to run after becoming a new mother and you shouldn't be doing it because you feel you must lose your baby weight and instantly snap back into shape. Rather, running at this time should be a means of helping you relax and have some time to yourself away from the demands of motherhood.

SENSIBLE TRAINING MEANT I RETURNED TO ELITE LEVEL A YEAR AFTER HAVING A BABY

Two-time Olympian and Commonwealth medallist LIZ YELLING, who has a marathon PB of 2 hours and 28 minutes, has a daughter, Ruby, and twins Sonny and Beau, with husband, Martin. Liz returned to run a marathon in 2 hours and 34 minutes two years after giving birth to Ruby, then retired from elite running before having her twins. The 40-year-old, who lives in Dorset, continues to run recreationally and coaches numerous athletes of all abilities [www.yellingperformance.com].

'As an elite athlete, I always followed a training plan targeting major races and championships. But during both of my pregnancies, following a set schedule went out the window.

'How I felt every day varied – sometimes I felt great and other days I felt drained. So I would never plan my training, I would head out the door when I felt up to it. I would never decide before I left how long I would run for – aside from the fact it would never be for longer than an hour. I would base how long I ran for on how I felt each time. If I felt good, I would run for an hour. If I didn't, I would just do half an hour or whatever I could manage.

'Running while pregnant gave me temporary relief from morning sickness, helped me to stay fit and managed my weight gain.

'Although I intended to resume my career as an elite athlete after I had my first baby, this was not a concern while I was pregnant. It's important to remember when expecting that you are not 'training' to get fitter, you are just running to be healthy for the birth and for your unborn child. It's a time when you should just be running because you enjoy it and because it makes you feel good. That's why it's very important to run how you feel – at a pace that's well within your capability – and scrap a training plan.

'My other advice to women running while pregnant is to be well fuelled and hydrated before your run so you are not relying on your energy reserves to get you through. Wear a bump support when you get bigger and run on ground with good footing so you are less likely to trip.

'Pregnancy is not a time to take risks. This meant I stopped running when I was 20 weeks pregnant with Ruby. At my 20-week scan, I discovered I had placenta previa. This is when the placenta lies low, blocking the womb opening. It can be observed in as many as one in three pregnancies at the 20-week stage. Its cause is not linked to exercising while expecting, but it does make a pregnancy more complicated as it increases the risk of bleeding. So I was advised just to walk and do low-impact activity for the rest of my pregnancy.

'After Ruby was born, I had two weeks of complete

rest. Then for the next fortnight I walked five to six times a week. For the next two weeks, I then ran/walked six times a week.

'Six weeks after labour, I could run non-stop for 30 minutes. During this time I was also vigilant about doing pelvic floor exercises to help my body recover from childbirth. At first running felt very sluggish and disjointed. It felt like the most unnatural thing to do at that time, and that I would have a lot of work to do to get fit again. However, I knew this wasn't the time to worry about achieving PBs or GB vests. When you become a new mum, it's important to take time to enjoy your new baby and set small, achievable running targets spread out over several months. If you build up very slowly, you are more likely to remain injury free. Your body will have a chance to heal from childbirth so it will be ready and able to handle increases in training when the time comes. Taking this cautious approach meant I was able to return to competing at an elite level a year after Ruby was born.

'When I became pregnant with the twins four years later, I had retired from elite competition but was still running to keep fit and be healthy – and because I love it. I was able to run until I was 18 weeks pregnant and then I got too large. I really suffered energy-wise and I knew there was nothing to be gained from trying to run when I was feeling heavy and tired.

'After the twins were born, I had a period of complete rest again. Then I started walking and first ran after four weeks for 20 minutes. I built the duration of my runs up very gradually over the following months until I could run for 6 miles two to four times a week. I enjoyed taking part in the Poole parkrun once a month.

'Life can be challenging as a full-time mum-of-three so I fit in running when I can. I don't have the flexibility to train that I had when I was an elite runner without children. In the first few months after having the twins, I just grabbed any 30 minute window to get out when the opportunity presented itself. This meant I ran two or three times a week at most, usually at the weekend when my husband had more time to look after the children.

'As soon as the twins were old enough to go in a running buggy, I had more opportunities to run. As Ruby was at school, it meant I could run after the school drop-off while pushing the twins.

'During the school holidays, it's harder for me to fit in running so I just take an easier week and enjoy the time with the children.'

Olympian: Liz Yelling returned to elite competition after having daughter Ruby – pic credit: www.helenturton.co.uk

EXERCISE & BREASTFEEDING

It's every mother's personal decision whether they want to breastfeed – and for how long. I was determined to breastfeed both my children so they could benefit from the nutrients and antibodies in breast milk and I was lucky it worked out well for me.

Women who want to keep fit may feel they have to stop breastfeeding earlier than non-active mums so they can resume an exercise regime, but you can do both. I ran a few times a week when I was breastfeeding Devon and Anya and I kept this up till they were more than a year old. Sometimes if I was out with them in the running buggy I would feed them mid-run in the park so they would feel settled and I could carry on running – a happy baby equals a happy mum.

Paula Radcliffe also breastfed her two children while still training hard (she won the New York Marathon 10 months after she had her daughter, Isla). She told me: 'I breastfed until six months and found it ok to combine this with hard training but I had to be really careful to eat enough and drink enough and had to store pumped milk for days when I was tired.'

Much of the apprehension over exercising while breastfeeding came from a study in the 1990s that found babies refused to drink milk that had been expressed as soon as their mothers had finished a hard workout. The reasoning was that lactic acid produced in the body when the women exercised at a high intensity gave the milk a bitter, unpalatable taste. This made some women fear that their babies would miss feeds if they exercised, which would restrict their growth and development as a result.

However, this study has since been widely discredited because the babies were fed by a stranger with a bottle and not by their mothers – which could have been the real reason why they didn't want to drink. More recent studies have found lactic acid will only affect the taste of breast milk if a mother exercises to exhaustion and then tries to breastfeed immediately after. I don't think there will be many mothers capable of pushing themselves to that extreme through exercise in the first six months of their baby's life if they are as lacking in energy and as sleep deprived as I was!

A separate follow-up study to the 1990s research concluded that exercise doesn't have a detrimental effect on breastfeeding. The article published in the Canadian Journal of Applied Physiology in 2001 states:

'Women should be advised that moderate exercise during lactation does not affect the quantity or composition of breast milk or impact infant growth.'

In another study two years later, researchers at the University of New Hampshire[5] agreed that exercise and breastfeeding are compatible and that physical activity can be beneficial for new mothers by helping them regain their pre-pregnancy figures and feel good about themselves. They state:

'Human studies suggest no detrimental effect of exercise during lactation on milk composition and volume, infant growth and development, or maternal health. Studies also demonstrate improved cardiovascular fitness in lactating, exercising women and suggest a quicker return to pre-pregnancy body weight and a more positive sense of wellbeing, compared to sedentary controls.'

Breastfeeding is thirsty work so if you are going to do it after exercising, make sure you drink extra water. If you chose to do extended breastfeeding like I did, then you might also find you are a little drained of energy so don't feel guilty about missing a run if you feel too tired.

You will most likely need a sports bra in a larger size then you wore before and might need to take extra precautions to prevent your nipples chafing at a time when they might already be engorged or sore. Do this by applying anti-chafing gels such as Vaseline or by wearing breast pads.

LABOUR WAS LIKE RUNNING A MARATHON!

VICKY DOHERTY lives in Lincoln with her husband, BJ, and their son, Harris. Here she explains how running enhanced her pregnancy and helped her through the pain of labour...

'As soon as I found out I was pregnant I stuck to easy running. I was so tired in the first few months holding back the pace wasn't a problem. I didn't have particularly bad morning sickness, whether or not this can be attributed in part to running, I couldn't say. I do think that it kept me generally fit, kept my core strong and prevented me from putting on unnecessary weight, all of which become pretty important in the later stages.

'I had already entered the White Peak Half Marathon in Matlock, which fell when I was 17 weeks pregnant, so I decided I would still take part but I would just run at a comfortable pace instead of racing. It was a nice, gentle off-road race with a downhill section so I really enjoyed it. I didn't look at my watch and listened to my body to ensure I wasn't pushing myself. I finished in 1 hour 56 minutes, which was 10 minutes outside my PB.

'Running up until the day of the half marathon was my aim, but as I still felt good I decided to carry on, taking each day at a time. In the end, that meant I kept going for another 17 weeks. When I started to show, it felt very odd having my belly bouncing around in front of me. However I quickly got used to the sensation and I noticed it less and less despite my bump getting bigger.

'Towards the end of my pregnancy, going for a run became quite liberating. Expectant mums are surrounded by people telling them to take it easy and put their feet up. I found it more relaxing to put my trainers on and go out for a gentle run where I could feel like myself for half an hour, rather than just being a heavily pregnant lady.

'Once I went into labour, I was glad I had maintained some fitness as you can't underestimate just how physically demanding childbirth is. I had to push for 2¼ hours. BJ was by my side treating it like an endurance event, feeding me 'Shot Bloks' (cubes similar to energy gels) and water on a strict schedule! I think the fact that I continued to run through my pregnancy meant that I had more stamina and more muscle tone where it mattered as you end up using your whole body to push. I think it was equally important that, as a runner, I knew how to push myself and continue pushing when I felt like I had nothing left. In that respect, labour is a lot like running a marathon. There's no question the pain was all worth it when our gorgeous son Harris arrived weighing 8lb 3oz.

'I didn't do any exercise at all until six weeks after his birth. I thought it would be really hard to wait that long to run again, but in actual fact there was no way my body was going to let me get back to it any sooner. The first few runs were much harder than I expected. To begin with, it was barely more than a walk, but it was wonderful to be out doing a couple of miles at any pace. Once Harris was five months old, I started to feel fit again and a few weeks after that I returned to my club's Tuesday evening group runs, which provided a great way to socialise, unwind and keep fit.'

Already done his first race: Vicky ran a half marathon while pregnant with her son, Harris

JUGGLING RUNNING & PARENTING

THIS SECTION APPLIES TO RUNNING DADS AS WELL AS MUMS!

Before I was a mother I could head out running whenever I felt like it, I sometimes wonder what I used to do with all my time before I had children! Now I barely have a minute to even have a shower in peace so fitting running in can be a struggle.

However, it's a lot easier to do than trying to go to the gym. As soon as I get a half-an-hour window, I can go out running and then be back on mum duty before I've even taken my trainers off.

I either have to plan ahead by getting up early and creeping out before the family wakes up or I'll get dressed into my running gear and then go spontaneously if and when the opportunity arises!

Using a running buggy once Devon and Anya turned six months old also gave me much more freedom to train. I use the BOB Ironman stroller, which doubles as a pushchair and has ample storage space. You can pop in hand weights or a skipping rope so it's like having your own mobile gym.

It's not recommended to take a baby in a running buggy until they are at least six months old and able to sit up by themselves. This is because their heads and necks are still delicate until this time and the reverberation from being in the buggy could make their heads bounce, causing neck and back injuries. This is why it's also important to invest in a proper running buggy when the time comes as they have been developed to have a better suspension than everyday strollers and are designed to move more smoothly. They will also have adequate cushioning for your child so they feel comfortable on the move, so much so that some running buggies can easily tackle off-road terrain. However, as you get used to running with a stroller, it's best to stick to smooth, flat paths.

Baby joggers are allowed in parkrun events so this is an excellent way to get you and your family out in the fresh air on a Saturday morning.

Once Devon and Anya were old enough to go in the baby jogger, I had a new lease of life. I was sometimes able to run five times a week and felt more like my old self again. It made it much easier to fit running into my day as I could use it if I was popping to the shops and run there and back instead of driving.

I found it was best to time the runs when the baby was tired and ready for a sleep so it would chill out in the pushchair and watch the world go by, or even doze off. Some runs could be stop and start as I'd have to pause to keep them entertained or let them snack on a rice cake, but it is such a great way to get mum (or dad) and baby out of the house. I often used it with Anya for the school run, running to pick up Devon with his scooter balanced on top of the buggy and then running back with him scooting beside me.

Remember, unless it's a hot day, it's important to keep babies in joggers wrapped up warm as they won't heat up like you will running.

TIPS FOR RUNNING PARENTS

Once your baby is six months old, get a running buggy. Try and test one before you buy to ensure you can run comfortably with it

Plan ahead so you can fit a run in before the family wakes up or when they've gone to bed

But also be ready to run at a moment's notice in case the opportunity arises

Take part in parkrun or junior parkrun during which you can run as a family or pushing a baby jogger

Make the school run a real school 'run' by running back after dropping them off or running there to pick them up

Be realistic about how much you can fit in. Don't beat yourself up if you can't train as often as you could before becoming a parent

Don't dwell on runs you've missed, but think about the fantastic runs that lie ahead

Don't feel like you are being selfish for wanting to go out running, remember you are setting your children an excellent example by keeping fit and healthy

Get your children involved. Take them to try a local running club or enter them in a fun run or junior parkrun

Lots of support on the day can be encouraging. It can be fun going to cheer on your family and friends. My son helped me start the Royal Parks Foundation Half Marathon and loved spotting all the runners in fancy dress

HOW TO GET YOUR CHILDREN RUNNING

Running is an excellent way to get children active, especially in the modern world where they are less likely to play out in the street with friends and often end up sitting around for hours watching TV or playing computer games.

Running clubs across the UK tend to accept children from age eight and up but check your local club for their age restrictions. Joining a club will provide children with the opportunity to have fun and make friends while keeping fit and healthy. There will be qualified coaches who will lead group sessions and

Lots of adult races have 'mini' runs so that the whole family can be involved

offer support and encouragement. If you join the same running club, you can also get fit along with your child.

When it comes to racing, there are fun runs across the country that children can take part in from an early age, as well as junior parkruns (www. parkrun.org.uk/events/juniorevents). These are free 2k-long timed runs for children aged four to 14 and their families.

Once they are old enough to join a running club, children will be given the opportunity to take part in track and cross-country events against other children their own age.

When children start running, they should build up how much they do gradually, as an adult would, and avoid high mileage while their bodies are still developing. Under 10s should avoid racing further than 2k and under 18s should only run up to 10k. Most road races have rules on the minimum age for entrants. To take part in a marathon in the UK, you must be at least 18. However, most coaches would agree that it's better for young people to focus on shorter distances, and progress to races like half marathons and marathons when they are older and stronger in their twenties and beyond.

MAKING TIME FOR ME

SARAH KINSELLA, 32, lives in Middlesex and is a full-time mum to Lara, four, and Anya, two. She loves to run for some 'me time'.

'I used to run when I was younger, then I stopped for a few years during which time I had my two daughters. I started running again when I became a full-time mum because I wanted to have some time just for me. When I go out for a run, it clears my head of any stress or worries so I come back reenergised for the children and the things I need to do around the house.

'Fitting in training is a bit of a juggling act but I always say "where there's a will there's a way". When my oldest is in school my youngest either comes with me in the running buggy or I run while she's in nursery or being looked after by a friend. If I take her in the running buggy, I time it with her nap and she falls straight to sleep.

'If I can't run during the day, I'll wait till my husband, Lorcan, gets home and go in the evening. I find it helps if I change into my running gear before he gets home so I'm ready to head out of the door as soon as he's back. Otherwise I can get too tired and it's more tempting to collapse on the couch!

'I often find on the days I'm exhausted and the last thing I want to do is head out for a run, that once I'm out I feel so reenergised and refreshed, it's always worth the effort.

'I love to regularly take part in races including my local parkrun. My husband often brings our children along to watch. It's a real motivator to have them there, especially hearing my four-year-old shouting "Go Mummy!" as I run past! It makes me feel really proud.'

Go Mum! Sarah's children love to support her at races

DEALING WITH STRESS INCONTINENCE

It's estimated that as many as one in three women in the UK suffer from stress incontinence – which is when urine involuntarily leaks out. Although it's a common problem, many suffer in silence because they are too embarrassed to talk about it. The issue may put some women off exercising altogether as leaks can frequently occur due to the downward pressure placed on the pelvic floor when running and jumping.

The pelvic floor muscles are responsible for supporting the bladder and urethra (the tube through which urine passes from the bladder to the outside). When these muscles are weak – which they often are after childbirth, during the menopause and in later life – embarrassing and unexpected leaks can occur. Some women find just laughing or sneezing can cause an accident because the pelvic floor muscles aren't strong enough. The good news is, it isn't something you

have to live with as it can be treated.

Physiotherapist Jean Johnson is a clinical specialist in women's health at Witty, Pask and Buckingham Physiotherapists (wpbphysio.co.uk) and has helped many women overcome stress incontinence. By following Jean's advice, stress incontinence shouldn't be a reason to give up exercise. If you do suffer from it, don't be afraid to seek further advice from your doctor or a physiotherapist like Jean who specialises in stress incontinence. Jean Johnson offers the following advice:

'The pelvic floor muscles are located in the base of the pelvis. If you sit on a firm chair, leaning forward, resting your elbows on your knees, you're sitting right on top of your pelvic floor muscles – this is the best position to take when first starting out on the strengthening exercises so you can feel them better. All women should get into the habit of exercising them daily in the following way: Squeeze the muscles around the back passage, vagina and opening to the bladder as firmly as you can, draw them up inside as if you're trying to stop yourself from passing urine, hold for as many seconds as you can up to 10 seconds. Relax the muscles, rest for 4 seconds, and then repeat as many times as you can up to a maximum of 10. Those who have been experiencing stress incontinence should do this three times a day. Once a day, everyone should also do up to 10 quicker, more pulse-type squeezes. These are designed to improve the coordination of your pelvic floor muscles, whereas the slow exercises are designed to improve the strength and stamina of your muscles. You can do pelvic floor exercises in any position and at any time, but avoid doing them in bed at night as the muscles will be tired so the exercises won't be as effective.'

Jean doesn't endorse this product but sufferers might also be interested in a company who have appeared on the TV show, Dragons' Den, called EVB Sport (evbsportsshorts.com). They have designed shorts specifically for sufferers of stress incontinence. The shorts have abdomen and pelvic support to prevent leaks. They also spare your blushes as, should you have an accident, they have a discreet integrated lining to hold a pad in place while you exercise. The shorts are made from moisture-wicking material with anti-bacterial treatments so you can remain comfortable.

RUNNING & THE MENOPAUSE

In Britain, the average age at which the menopause is experienced is 51. But some symptoms and hormonal changes can begin earlier than that. Some women will go through 'the change' without experiencing many difficulties, while for others, hot flushes, mood swings and an inability to sleep will make them feel miserable. It's also a time when some women may feel less confident, with fears over loss of youth and sex appeal bringing them down.

During the menopause, women stop producing certain hormones – including oestrogen – which cause the menstrual cycle and allow them to bear children. The loss of oestrogen is detrimental because it protects bones from calcium deficiency – which is why older women are more at risk of osteoporosis. Oestrogen also aids the relaxation of blood vessels in the heart, which is why post-menopausal women are at more risk of heart, problems, and it keeps the bladder and urethra healthy, so without it stress incontinence (as explained on pages 136–137) is more likely.

However, there is a way for women to stay healthy and feel confident, strong and happy through their menopause and beyond. You guessed it, running is again the answer! In 2012, researchers at the University of Granada, Spain, found that menopausal women who undertook an exercise programme felt physically and mentally better than those who did not[6]. The study, published in the Journal of Clinical Nursing, concluded: 'Menopausal women may benefit from physical exercise, which attenuates the effects of the physiological and psychological changes associated with the menopause and prevents pathologic changes.' The study also found that exercise at this time in a woman's life can enhance their overall quality of life.

Running will make the heart healthy, while lifting weights has been found to increase muscle mass and bone density (see more on this on pages 86–87) so women over 50 should do this regularly to prevent osteoporosis. See pages 54–55 for advice on pumping iron.

It's never too late to take up running and women who do so during the menopause will be able to curtail any associated weight gain and feel good about themselves instead of 'past it'. Many women in their fifties can out-run women half their age – like Treena Johnson, from my home county of Yorkshire, who achieved a time of 2 hours and 57 minutes at the 2014 London Marathon at the age of 52.

So if you are already a runner, keep on running through your menopause to carry on feeling fit and good about yourself. Or if you want to start running in your fifties, follow our beginners' 5k training plan at the start of the book and read the 'running as you age' section in Chapter 3 for further tips.

HOW HAZEL BECAME FABULOUSLY FIT IN HER FIFTIES

HAZEL PONSFORD, from Berkshire, took up exercise at the age of 50 and she's never felt better...

'At 54, I'm the fittest I've ever been. In the past four years, I have run three half marathons, qualified to be a Pilates instructor and I can lift 35kg weights.

'It all started the month before I turned 50. I was looking for a new challenge and a colleague suggested running. I started training and after a couple of months, I completed two 5ks. I then did a 10k and a half marathon. I was amazed that I had been able to complete 13.1 miles in my 50th year.

'I carried on running, improving my half marathon PB, and then started focusing on high-intensity interval workouts – as well as using weights – as I wanted to tone up. I followed an exercise plan recommended by personal trainer Julia Buckley in her book The Fat Burn Revolution.

'I began lifting small weights and used heavier ones as I got stronger. Now I use dumbbells ranging from 3kg to 12.5kg, or I lift 35kg in total when using a bar.

'Lifting weights is a wonderful way to stay healthy as you age. You will not "bulk up" but gain lean muscle. If you're afraid of lifting and think you can't, consider how heavy your handbag/child/shopping is – you lift those without thinking about it.

'Exercise has definitely given me greater self-confidence in my fifties. For example, I have trained to become a Pilates instructor. I would never have had the confidence to stand in front of a group of people and lead them when I was younger.

'I am currently in the peri-menopause phase. Whether or not regular exercising has helped keep menopausal symptoms to a minimum is difficult to say, but I like to think that the ease I'm experiencing is due, at least in part, to being so active.

'Exercise has made me happy with, and within, my body and I want to remain fit and healthy as I face the remainder of my fifties and beyond. Women my age shouldn't be afraid to start exercising, you're never too old to try something new. Remember that however slow you are running, you are still faster than those sat on the sofa.'

Never say never! Hazel is proof that you are never too old to take up exercise

BEAUTY ON THE RUN

I think it's sad when I hear many young girls and women are put off exercising because they are worried about how they will look. They fear they will appear unattractive and unfeminine when red-faced and sweaty. But I think this is nonsense. The way I see it, exercising gives you a healthy glow and colour in your cheeks. Running will make your body stronger and healthier, which will give you better skin and shinier hair.

I wanted to maximise awareness for my chosen charity, Cancer Research UK

Annoyingly, women are constantly judged on their appearance, especially as we get older. Men can accumulate wrinkles and grey hair and are told they look wise and distinguished. Yet women are told they look old and frumpy or have 'let themselves go'.

Rather than appearance, I think it's more worthwhile to focus on health and fitness – which in turn helps people look and feel younger for longer. It's a much better use of your energy than fretting about how you look or spending money on anti-ageing creams and cosmetic surgery.

When it comes to body shape, I think it's much better for young women to aspire to be fit than thin. Athletes like Jessica Ennis-Hill make much better role models than some skinny celebrities.

By keeping fit, you don't have to worry about starving yourself to stay trim and you'll become toned instead of bony. Eating healthy foods full of vitamins like avocado will also boost the appearance of your skin.

I'm flattered if people say I still manage to look good when I'm racing, but I am more concerned with how I feel and how I perform than my

appearance when I'm running. So I don't really have many beauty tips other than sleeping and eating well to enhance your appearance and drinking lots of water every day. When it comes to beauty products, I avoid any with too many chemicals and go for more natural ones. I like Green People (www.greenpeople.co.uk) who do organic products for men and women. I'm also a fan of Daniel Sandler's products. He's a professional make-up artist (and now a friend) I have been lucky to work with over the years.

I wouldn't recommend piling on the make-up when running as it will clog up your pores and only run off when you sweat. If you do want to wear mascara then make sure it's waterproof so it doesn't end up running down your face if you get caught in the rain or if you get emotional at the finish line!

Wash the sweat off your face as soon as you can after running (you could pack wet wipes to use after races) to prevent spots.

Lip balm is a good idea to prevent your lips drying out and you can get tinted ones if you want to add a bit of colour to your face. There are other little things you can do to enhance your look or make you feel more feminine when running such as having your eyebrows shaped or painting your nails.

The most important thing when running if you want to protect your face against ageing (not to mention skin cancer) is to wear a moisturiser with high SPF protection or a high-factor sunscreen. I love coconut oil as it's so soothing and nourishing to lather on the face and body after a post-run bath/shower.

Finally, if you're really concerned about looking good when you see a photographer taking your picture during a race – just remember to smile!

6: THE ULTIMATE CHALLENGE – RUNNING A MARATHON

144

ARE YOU READY?

Completing a marathon is the ultimate feat for many runners and is a challenge that shouldn't be taken on lightly. While humans have evolved to run, we haven't been designed to run as far as 26.2 miles.

So, whether you are a 3- or 5-hour marathoner, making it to the finish of any marathon is a huge achievement. It can also be an agonising and painful experience – but it is worth it – and there are steps you can take to prevent race-day disasters and to avoid hitting the dreaded 'wall'.

The allure of the marathon attracts many because it's the ultimate test of your fitness and grit. It's an experience as well as a race – you'll feel a rollercoaster of emotions from beginning to end including excitement at the start, fatigue in the middle and elation at finishing. The support at big-city marathons like London creates a carnival atmosphere that it's wonderful to be part of, and running a marathon is an excellent way to raise money and awareness of different charities.

While for some running one marathon is enough, for others (like myself!) it can become addictive and you want to keep trying to beat your previous time and learn from past mistakes.

I love the marathon, but I'm also fully aware of what an endeavour it is. So while I encourage all runners to give it a go at least once, I would also advise thinking carefully before committing. You should sign up when you are injury-free and have the time to dedicate to the training. You need to fully prepare yourself for the race with at least 12 weeks of training so your body can handle the distance. So if you're ready to take on the challenge, here's my advice on how to do it.

MARATHON JARGON

TAPERING:

Running fewer miles in the last three weeks before the race so you feel fresher on race day.

CARB-LOADING:

Eating extra carbohydrates in the build up to the race to avoid hitting the wall.

HITTING THE WALL:

Becoming so energy depleted, you struggle to keep running and can't maintain a pace that was easy at the start.

MILE SPLITS:

The time it takes you to run each mile in the race.

NEGATIVE SPLIT:

Running faster in the second half of the race than the first.

TRAINING ESSENTIALS

SEE RUNNING SCHEDULES ON P180

Whether you are a beginner or a more experienced runner, it's advisable to have a 12–15-week build-up to the marathon. During this time, you should gradually increase your mileage.

When you first get a place in a marathon, which is often a year or six months before the event, it can be tempting to get carried away and try to train hard immediately. But this could lead to you doing too much, too soon and then becoming injured. It's better to keep your fitness ticking over at a lower mileage and then start building up your marathon training 12 weeks from race day. This means your hardest training, longest runs and highest weekly mileage will fall three to five weeks before race day itself.

With three weeks to go, you should then gradually decrease your training – known as tapering – so your body can adapt and recover from the training and be fresh for the 26.2 mile race on marathon day.

Further on in this chapter, I reveal the training I did to run sub-three. At the back of the book, you will find training plans that experienced runner and Great North Run pace maker, Alan Dent (pictured left), has kindly provided for beginners, intermediates and more advanced runners. Alan took up running when he was 24 and, after joining Blaydon Harriers Athletics Club in Gateshead, PBs he clocked up include a half marathon of 1 hour 16 minutes and that marathon of 2 hours 49 minutes.

Whether you a beginner, or a more experienced distance runner, a key component of any marathon training plan is a weekly long run. It is vital because it gets you used to being on your feet for a long time and teaches your body to store and use fuel to keep you going.

It also gives you an opportunity to practise for the race to avoid problems on the day. For example, you should practise what food you will eat the night before and test which energy gels or

Alan Dent regularly runs off road

drinks you will take on during the run to ensure you don't get an upset stomach and are hydrated enough to keep going. You should also practise running in your race kit and trainers to ensure they are comfortable – particularly important if you choose to run in fancy dress!

Most training plans advocate a long run of up to 20 miles. You shouldn't be running this distance at the start of your training, but build up to it each week. You can either measure your run by distance if you have a GPS watch, or by time. Then gradually increase the distance each week by a mile or two, or the time by 10–15 minutes. A tip I read in Richard Nerurkar's excellent book, *Marathon Running*, is that for advanced runners, your five longest runs in the build-up to the marathon should total 100 miles. This is what I aimed for when training for my sub-three marathon.

Your longest run should be three or four weeks before the marathon. For beginners, 20 miles is sufficient. More experienced runners could try getting up to 22–24 miles. It is not recommend to run 26 miles before race day unless you are a seasoned elite athlete (and even they won't cover this distance in one go that often in training). It takes your body a long time to recover from a 26-mile run so doing it in training could tire you out or injure you before the big day. It's far better to save running 26 miles till race day when your body will go into the event well-rested and prepared.

Interval sessions are still important when marathon training to add variety to your schedule and to give your body a harder workout to make you fitter. Once a week you could do sessions as recommended by Liz Yelling earlier in the book (page 42), or intervals such as 5–6 x 1 mile, 6 x 1K or 8 x 800m. You don't need to run these intervals flat out, but you should be going faster than your target marathon pace, so you might be running at your half marathon or 10k pace.

If you are determined to run a specific time, then learning to run at your target marathon pace is also important. Look at the pace chart at the back of the book (pages 178–179) and you can work out your target pace per mile based on a previous race time or the finishing time you hope to achieve. Be realistic about your goal and your capabilities in line with how hard you are prepared to train. Many people believe one good way to estimate the marathon time you are capable of is to double your half marathon time and then add 10 minutes. This works out for me as in 2012 I ran a half marathon of 1 hour, 21 minutes and 51 seconds, and I then ran the marathon in 2 hours, 54 minutes.

If it's your first marathon, then don't put too much pressure on yourself to run a certain time. It will be an unknown so just focus on getting around. It's a real learning curve so you might realise after your first one that you have to pace it better or take on more fuel.

Knowing your target marathon pace – and sticking to it – is important if you want to run to the best of your ability. The most efficient – and comfortable – way to run a marathon is at an even pace from beginning to end. Fit and experienced runners try and achieve a 'negative split' – running faster in the second half than the first. However, this is difficult to achieve as it means holding yourself back at the start of the race when your marathon pace feels too easy and then having enough energy reserves to increase your pace towards the end, so it may be best to avoid doing this.

Tower Bridge is one of the many highlights of the London Marathon course

148

Most amateur marathon runners end up running much faster in the first half than the second and as a result, many 'hit the wall' or 'blow up', meaning they can't handle the pace any more and get slower and slower. Often this happens as people believe if they go off fast they will then have banked time, so if they slow in the second half they should still achieve their target time. However, this is rarely the case as if you go off too fast, you are more likely to struggle in the second half and lose much more time than you gained. Therefore it's better to try to stick to your target pace from the start. I know it isn't easy as it's so tempting to go faster in the first 6 miles when you are full of adrenaline and feel fresh and comfortable and you can get swept along by the crowds and excitement. But by holding yourself back, you are much more likely to achieve your target finishing time.

Wearing a GPS watch is a great way to monitor your pace and ensure you're not running too fast at the beginning of the race. If you don't have one, use a stopwatch and make a mental note of your time through each mile marker. Some watches will allow you to do laps whereby you save every mile you have run and the timer restarts so you can ensure you are running the correct pace each mile. Or if you only have a stopwatch that runs continuously, you should work out what time you need to reach each mile in (see the pace chart at the back of the book), for example, for 8-minute mile pace: 2 miles would be 16 minutes, 10 miles would be 80 minutes, etc. It can be hard to remember all these figures so you can make your own, or search online, for a wristband that you can write your target times on and then print off. On the day, you can glance at the figures on your wristband to check you are on target as you pass the mile markers.

Learning to run at your target marathon pace in training is important as it will get you used to how it feels so you are more able to slot into that pace on the day. It also teaches your body how to run at that speed. You could either intersperse some marathon pace running into your weekday runs, or try to do some of your long runs at marathon pace (it's not recommended to do the entire duration of your long runs at marathon pace though, as this could tire you out for the rest of the week's training).

If you are serious about doing a marathon and want to run it to the best of your ability, then you will have to make training a priority. This might mean making some sacrifices or neglecting some other areas of your life for a few weeks – for me it was the housework! I didn't have the time or energy to do it when I was also trying to run 90 miles a week. You might have to forgo some nights on the town with friends (it's never a good idea to try and do a long run with a hangover!) or delay a family holiday until after the race. Hopefully your friends and family will be supportive if they know how much completing a marathon means to you – and it's only for 12 weeks, which will soon fly by.

Running well in the marathon isn't just about getting the training in though. You'll also need to maintain a good diet (see the Food For Fuel chapter) and make sure you get plenty of sleep so your body can recover and adapt to the training. Also, make sure you get regular sports massages to loosen tight muscles and keep injury at bay.

COMBATING THE LONELINESS OF THE LONG-DISTANCE RUNNER

Training for a marathon can mean doing lots of running on your own. But it doesn't have to be that way. Here are a few tips on how you can share your journey with like-minded people.

LISTEN TO MARATHON TALK

This is a free podcast recorded every week by runners Martin Yelling and Tom Williams, bringing marathon-related news, tips, amusing stories and interviews with top runners. I'm a huge fan of the show and have been lucky enough to guest present it. You can download it so you can listen to it on the run to keep you motivated and entertained. They also have a Facebook page where you can connect with other marathon runners to share advice and gain support (www.facebook.com/ marathontalk). To listen to, or download, the podcast, visit www.marathontalk.com.

JOIN A RUNNING CLUB

Meet some fellow marathoners at your local running club who you can link up with for long runs and support. Most clubs have runners of all abilities so you should be able to find others who are your pace to run with. The long runs will certainly fly by with company and could help you discover interesting new routes.

TAKE A FRIEND

If you have a friend or family member who can run, take them with you. Even if they don't want to run as far as you do, if they join you for half of your long run it will break it up for you and help the time go by faster. If they are not a runner, perhaps they could join you on a bike and cycle beside you to make conversation and pass you a water bottle when you need a drink.

ENTER A 20-MILE RACE

There are various 20-mile races held in the build-up to spring marathons. I've enjoyed doing the Spen 20 in Yorkshire when I've been training for London. A 20-mile race is a great way to gain confidence, practise your race routine and get a long run in with other people on a measured route. However, try not to run a 20-mile race too hard as that could mean it takes you longer to recover. It's better to save your best race effort for marathon day, so if you do a 20-mile race within five to three weeks of your marathon, try to take it steady rather than run it as fast as you can.

WRITE A BLOG

Writing about your marathon journey is an effective way to keep a record of your experience and to inspire other people. You can use it to share what you've learnt along the way and as a means of connecting with other marathon runners by inviting them to leave comments.

SOCIAL NETWORK

Social media like Twitter and Facebook offer an opportunity to follow and communicate with runners from novices to elite athletes and will help you feel part of the friendly, global running community. It's a wonderful way to share advice and gain support. You can find me at @nell_ mcandrew on Twitter.

GETTING A PLACE IN THE LONDON MARATHON

The London Marathon is so popular there aren't enough places for the number of people who want to run it every year. As a result, they hold a ballot to allocate entries. The ballot for the next race usually opens one to two weeks after the race has been held each year and closes as soon as the entry limit is reached – which usually only takes a few hours.

Entries must be made via the London Marathon website (virginmoneylondonmarathon.com) and then entrants find out in October if they got in. Aside from the ballot, there are others ways to gain entry. If you have run a particularly quick time in a previous marathon, you can apply for a 'good for age' or 'championship place'. Visit the London Marathon website for up-to-date details on the qualifying times.

Running clubs are allocated a number of places so joining your local club could give you a shot at earning a place that way, depending on how they are distributed. Some clubs hold their own ballots or have a first come, first served system.

Charities have a number of spaces and by signing up to run for them you can raise some money for a good cause. They can also help you to arrange your accommodation and transport to the race and offer support and encouragement in the build-up and on the day. But be warned, you usually have to commit to raising a sizable sum of around £2,000.

If you aren't lucky enough to get a place in London, then remember there are plenty of other equally amazing marathons around the world you can enjoy instead. Other major races like the Berlin Marathon also have a ballot entry system but smaller, local races won't fill up so quickly. New marathons are starting up all the time – in the UK, Brighton, Manchester, Bournemouth and Yorkshire are just a few that have been established in recent years. Most races must be entered months in advance so do an Internet search to establish which one you want to target in the future and check the race website for details on how you can enter.

TAPERING

Your longest run should take place at least three weeks before race day. After that, you should gradually decrease your mileage to 80 per cent, then 60 per cent, and 30 per cent for the final three weeks before race day. This means that during the week before the race you should be doing hardly any running except some short, gentle runs. If you do want to keep your legs ticking over, you could do a short marathon-paced run or intervals (no more than three miles) at the start of the week.

Resting at this time can be difficult as you'll find it strange to be doing nothing after fitting in so much training for the past few months. But doing nothing is actually hugely important when it comes to tapering. It gives your body a chance to recover from all the hard training you have been doing, so you'll be fresh and full of energy on the start line. It means your body will have adequate glycogen stores – which you can top up by carb-loading in the final few days before the race (see the Food For Fuel chapter on pages 96–97 for more on this).

It can sometimes be difficult to do less training once you are in a routine of high mileage. You might also worry that you will lose fitness by training less or that your body will have forgotten how to run by race day. But don't panic. Trust in the training you have done and enjoy sitting back and putting your feet up. Remember, in the last two weeks before the race any hard training you do will not make a difference to your fitness on the day. So rather than trying to cram in extra miles, which could make you tired, it's better to do less so you will be refreshed and rejuvenated in time for the race.

The day before the race it's particularly important not to spend too much time on your feet. So if you are going to an exhibition to collect your number, don't wander around the stalls for too long. Also, avoid the temptation to do other jobs you haven't had time to do when you've been training, like DIY around the house or mowing the lawn. Let it wait another few days till after the race.

Try to get some early nights in the week before the race. It's normal not to be able to sleep that well the night before as you'll be full of nerves and excitement. So if you have banked some good nights' sleep earlier in the week you shouldn't be adversely affected by one relatively sleepless night.

MY MARATHON RACE DAY TIPS

FUEL UP

You should have been carb-loading in the preceding days and had a carb-heavy meal the night before the race (make sure it's a dish you've had the night before a long run before so you're sure it agrees with you). Then have a good breakfast 2–3 hours before the run, such as porridge or toast with jam.

AVOID CHAFING

Bleeding nipples are a common and painful sight on many runners. Avoid them by applying anti-chafing gels to your body in the morning before you put your kit on and topping up just before the race in any delicate areas. Men could also try putting plasters over their nipples as theirs are more prone to bleeding than women's. Also, cover your feet in anti-chafing gel to prevent blisters and apply gel to anywhere else your clothes might rub.

HYDRATE

Drink a couple of glasses of water before the race but don't go overboard. It's dangerous to drink too much and will mean you have a stomach full of water and need frequent toilet stops. Adjust how much you drink to how hot it is on the day. Once the race is underway, don't wait till you're thirsty to have a drink, but sip water little and often.

KNOW THE COURSE

Familiarise yourself with the route in advance. This could help you mentally tick off the miles. You can also plan where your friends and family will stand so you can look out for them when you run past.

PLAN AHEAD

You don't want to waste nervous energy on the morning of the race worrying about the practicalities so make sure you have planned your journey to the start line in advance, allowing plenty of time to get there. Familiarise yourself with the organisation at the event so you know how and where your kit will be stored and agree a specific place near the finish where you can meet your loved ones afterwards.

KEEP WARM

Take some spare clothing or a bin bag to wear that you can then discard on the start line, as you often have to hand in your clothes for baggage storage at least 30 minutes before the off. I also highly recommend wearing spare trainers to arrive in, as at the London Marathon the grass at Greenwich Park is usually damp early in the morning. Then if it rains during the race you'll also have a dry pair to change into at the finish.

DON'T GO OFF TOO FAST!

Find out what pace per mile you need to run to achieve your target time (see the pace chart on pp. 178–179) and stick to it. It can be tempting to get carried away with the race atmosphere and run too quickly at the beginning, but it's better to run an even-paced race if you want to avoid 'hitting the wall'.

WRITE YOUR NAME ON YOUR VEST

This is a great way to gain some extra support from the crowds. Hearing them cheer your name will help keep you going if you start to tire.

RECOVERY

Running a marathon puts a huge strain on your whole body and causes many micro tears in your muscles. To aid your recovery, get some warm clothes on as soon as you can after the finish and eat or drink some protein.

The day after the marathon it's completely normal to find you can't walk without considerable pain! Trying to get up and down stairs will be particularly difficult. This muscle soreness should wear off after a few days. In the meantime, have some hot baths and try to get a sports massage to relieve some of the tension in your muscles.

You could try some 'active recovery' later in the week such as walking, cycling or swimming, but avoid running. Plan to take a few days – or a whole week – off doing any running at all. When you do resume training, start off with some short, gentle runs and avoid speed work for a couple of weeks. If you want to continue running once you've run a marathon, then it's important not to overdo any training at this time as you could become injured by pushing yourself too hard when your body is still recovering from the marathon.

To this end, it's also important not to do too many marathons in the same year. You might be on a high after finishing and keen to do another one. Or if it didn't go well, you might want to try to find another race as soon as possible to try to redeem yourself. However you won't be doing your body any favours by rushing into another marathon. You are also unlikely to run well because you won't be fully recovered from the first one, so it's better to wait –

even if you have the 'post-marathon blues'. This can happen because you have been so focused on the marathon for so long and then experience such a high at achieving your goal, that afterwards you may feel a bit flat and demotivated. Despite this, it's not good to immediately target another marathon to get the buzz back. Instead, once you have recovered, there are plenty of other challenges you could take on, such as trying to get a faster 5k or 10k time or doing some off-road races.

You could target another marathon in the future,

but it's advisable to wait at least six months. This is why most big city marathons fall in the spring or autumn to allow athletes to recover in between and peak in their training to run well on the day.

A 2014 study found there's another serious reason why you should avoid multiple marathons a year, or for too many years in succession. Running has been widely proven to be beneficial for heart health and many more people die from heart problems related to a sedentary lifestyle than from running. However, the research published in the Journal of the Missouri State Medical Association found that men who had run a marathon a year for 25 years had an accelerated chance of developing heart disease[1]. As a result, they advise running in moderation to gain the many health benefits without causing heart damage.

So, with this in mind, stick to targeting certain races and training hard for them for a set number of weeks, rather than training hard all year round. Remember, the many benefits of running far outweigh the negatives, but it's important to train and race sensibly and listen to medical advice. Not only that, after all the hard training you've done for the marathon, it's good to give yourself time to do other things and catch up on the jobs (and with the people) you may have neglected in your pursuit of marathon glory.

TIPS ON RAISING SPONSORSHIP MONEY

Charities can get guaranteed places in some major races, but require commitment to raise money in return for the chance to race. It's increasingly difficult to raise money in hard economic times and if you regularly want to race and raise money for charity, you may find it tricky to keep asking the same friends and family for donations. But there are lots of ways to do it, especially by using modern technology to help.

First of all, set up an online page, such as JustGiving, to make it easy for people to donate online. Spread the word about what you are doing via social media.

Could you do something different to make your challenge stand out, such as race in fancy dress, or go for a World Record as the fastest vegetable/ school girl etc?! The possibilities seem endless! I have run in fancy dress on numerous occasions, such as Bat Girl and a fairy. It's good fun and a wonderful way to draw more attention to your cause. Just remember to think through your costume carefully to make sure it's comfortable. Practise running in it before race day and liberally apply anti-chafing gel where it could rub – for example around your neck if you're wearing a cape (I learnt this the hard way!)

Contact your local newspaper to see if they would be interested in covering your story and include a call-out for sponsorship. If you work for a large company, you could ask your employer if they would be interested in sponsoring you.

You could also drum up some extra donations by organising events such as a jumble sale, cake sale or by hosting a quiz and asking teams to make a donation to enter. You could also see if local businesses would be interested in donating prizes so you can then hold a fundraising raffle or auction. For example, ask a local salon if they could donate a prize of a free haircut, or a sports masseur to promise a free massage.

Set up a blog and share the highs and lows of your training – that way people can see how much effort you are putting in to achieve your goal and how much you deserve the sponsorship money.

People like to know how their money makes a difference so tell them how your charity can use their donation – sometimes just a small amount like £5 can be enough to save a life if it pays for a vaccination etc.

Lee McQueen and I ran for Cancer Research UK at the Great North Run

MY MARATHON JOURNEY

Even though I was relatively fit in my twenties, making the decision to run a marathon in 2004 was a massive step for me. Having grown up watching the London Marathon on TV, I was always in awe of all the participants, from the elite athletes pushing for world record times at the front, to the charity runners taking part against the odds.

The stories of the people involved always moved me and I knew one day I'd love to take part in support of a worthwhile cause. But at the back of my mind I always wondered 'could I really run 26.2 miles?' and I never had the guts to enter. Then I met Epidermolysis Bullosa sufferer Jonny Kennedy – and it was making a promise to him to take part that meant I had to go for it.

I met Jonny through the charity DebRA, which supports people in the UK with the rare, genetic skin condition Epidermolysis Bullosa (EB). Sufferers can get severe blistering and intense pain from the slightest touch, so many find the day-to-day activities we take for granted impossible, and they aren't even able to hold hands with, or hug, their loved ones.

In the summer of 2003, DebRA invited me to an event in London's Hyde Park where children with the condition and their parents were going to release butterflies. The delicate wings of the insects are symbolic for the charity, representing the fragility of the EB sufferers' skin. I was privileged and humbled to meet the adorable children whose bodies had to be covered in bandages as they played in the park.

Jonny, a 36-year-old EB sufferer who was from the North like me, was at the event and asked to meet me. He was joined by a film crew who were following him for a documentary – 'The Boy Whose Skin Fell Off' – which you may have seen on Channel 4. He was covered in blisters and could only move thanks to a wheelchair, but I remember how smart he looked in his shirt, waistcoat and hat. He was witty, intelligent and very open about his 36 years of suffering. He had to have his bandages changed daily and the condition had made his fingers completely fuse together. The slightest touch brought him immense pain, and to top it all, he'd just been diagnosed with skin cancer.

He related his terrible symptoms with such self-deprecating humour that I was moved to tears. He told me he had done everything within his capabilities to raise money and awareness for DebRA – including a blister-inducing trolley dash, and giving up his privacy so camera crews could film him for the documentary as he faced his terminal cancer diagnosis.

He wanted to do whatever he could to find a cure and I was determined to help him. I can't remember how the marathon came into the

conversation, but the next thing I knew I was promising Jonny I would run the next London Marathon for DebRA and raise as much money as I could in the process. He promised he would be there to meet me at the finish line – but sadly this wasn't to be. Not long after we met, Jonny died. I knew when we met he was dying, but I suppose I didn't realise how soon that would happen.

I was determined to fulfil my promise to him and complete the marathon in his memory. But I didn't just want to finish, I wanted to do it to the best of my ability and raise as much money as I could in the process. As well as DebRA, I chose to run for some other charities close to my heart – Cancer Research UK, the Lymphoma Association and SSAFA (National Armed Forces Charity). I chose these charities because my Dad had just been treated for non-Hodgkins lymphoma and I have been privileged to meet many of our brave troops as a 'forces' sweetheart'. I've seen first hand what a difference these charities can make to people's lives and wanted to help.

To run a marathon, I knew I would have to train a lot more than I was used to and push myself beyond just running on the treadmill for half an hour.

I trained through the winter even if it was cold, wet and windy. I built up the distance of my long run every Sunday until I could run for 18 miles. I wasn't running a high weekly mileage – probably around 30–40 miles a week – but I was also doing cross training in the gym, lifting weights and doing exercise classes like Boxerise.

I still had doubts about whether I was capable of running the marathon, but joining Thames Valley Harriers at my friend Alison's suggestion was a real turning point (read more on this in Chapter 2, pages

Meeting Jonny made me realise that anything was possible. If he could put himself through challenges whilst being in so much discomfort, there was no excuse for me not to be able to run the London Marathon. I will never forget you Jonny

YOUR MARATHON TIPS

**Here's some excellent advice
from my Twitter followers...**

Count down the miles rather than up (Anthony Judge @Ant_Judge)

Stick to your pace, overtaking people from mile 20 onwards gives you more confidence than slowing down. Take water at every station and enjoy the day! Don't listen to music, listen to people cheering. Finally, dedicate a mile to someone, e.g. 18-19 your mum (Mr Kev @MrKev1980)

Don't stop, just keep running! (Louise Phillips @LouP252)

Plan to enjoy it but be prepared to push yourself too (Sarah Dudgeon @ArtOfYrSuccess)

Eat well the night before the big race but be careful not to overeat to avoid unexpected issues (Natalie Teece @natteece)

All the hard work's done, enjoy the day (Tim Wilsher @polliehops)

Pace yourself, don't rush off too fast, and anything can happen on the day, go with your head and your heart (Nikki @nikki2777)

Smile for the camera at the finish! (Tony Airey @flippingdiscs)

Make sure your five long runs total 100 miles, as read in Richard Nerurkar's book (Glenn Still @064214)

You've spent a lot of hours training hard. Enjoy your race, you've earned it (Cath @rookcie)

Don't go off too fast, slowly slowly catchy monkey (Mark Peach @peachy6211)

Do the training. Know your pace. Set realistic time goals. Don't make time your enemy on the day! (Neil Vickery @NeilBVickery)

47–48). Running with the other club members and getting their advice and support raised my confidence as well as my fitness.

In the build-up to London, I ran the Reading Half Marathon in 1 hour 32 minutes and then did my first 20-miler – a race called the Spen 20 in Cleckheaton, Yorkshire. It was tough as it was raining, it was windy and the route consisted of a number of steep hills. There were no cheering crowds and no medal at the finish, but I was delighted to complete the route in 2 hours and 38 minutes. It had been physically and mentally challenging, but I knew I was now ready for the big one in a month's time. I tapered my training over the next few weeks so I was fully recovered from the Spen 20 and had fresh legs for marathon day.

The week of the race arrived and despite all the training, I was filled with self-doubt. I worried I wouldn't be able to manage the distance and that if I failed, I would let everyone down – myself, the charities, Jonny, my friends and family and everyone who had given me so much support. What if I were to get cramp, or need the loo? All these thoughts were spinning around in my mind. I couldn't sleep the night before the race as I was so nervous. When I finally nodded off, I dreamt I took a wrong turn on the course and got lost! I woke up that morning feeling tired and full of nervous expectation. When I arrived at Greenwich Park the atmosphere was electric and people were in high spirits even though it was a wet and miserable day. I could tell many were as nervous as I was. When we were called to the 'green' start line it was still drizzling with rain so I wore a black bin liner over my vest and shorts to keep a bit warmer until the race began. As I waited nervously, I started chatting to a fellow runner – Jim McDonnell. As I mentioned previously in the book, he's an ex-professional boxer with a marathon PB of 2 hours 50 minutes. We chatted about what training we had done and he reassured me that I would make it round and I would even enjoy it! He said if I wanted to up my training for the following year, I should give him a call. But I couldn't think about doing it again at that point, just doing it once would be enough! The announcer then said we had a minute to go so I took off the bin liner and wished Jim good luck. Then there was a 10-second countdown, and we were off!

The support around the whole course was amazing and is what makes London one of the greatest marathons in the world. The route passes Cutty Sark, over Tower Bridge, round Canary Wharf and down the Embankment to Big Ben before passing Buckingham Palace to finish on The Mall. There isn't a section without crowd support and in some spots the cheering is so loud it's deafening. It really helps you keep going when your whole body feels like it can't carry on. That, and the other runners around you who support and encourage one another, which can bring the best out in you. It's no wonder the London Marathon is over-subscribed every year because so many people want to take part and experience the carnival atmosphere while striving to achieve what seems impossible.

When the going got tough, I thought of the charities I was raising money for and of how ill my dad had been while having chemotherapy. If he could fight cancer, I could battle on to the end of the race, no matter how tired I felt.

The huge sense of achievement after completing the marathon is overwhelming

Finishing a marathon is an emotional experience, you are drained physically and emotionally. When I crossed the line I burst into tears – but they were happy tears. I was delighted I had been able to finish in a time of 3 hours 22 minutes – all the hard work had paid off. Thanks to the people who had sponsored me – including *The Sun* newspaper – I raised £50,000 for charity. I had also fulfilled my promise to Jonny. I just wish he had been there to see it.

At some point in the marathon most people always think, 'why am I doing this?' and 'never again!' But they soon change their minds when their aching bodies start to recover and stairs can be walked up and down again with ease. I was no different, so the day after my first marathon, even though I was so stiff I could barely walk, I kept thinking, 'Maybe I could do it again and next time I could go faster!'

So after much consideration, I signed up to do London again the following year, raising money for the same charities.

I would be delighted to take part in the New York, Paris or Dubai Marathons one day, but I chose to do London again as it is currently my home and I love the route and atmosphere.

By the January, I was ready to resume my marathon training so it was back to weekly sessions and back to doing long Sunday runs. I also did three other runs a week of 6–15 miles. I knew I would have to train harder if I wanted to run faster, so I decided to take up Jim's offer of help. I nervously called him hoping he would remember me and he said he'd be delighted to help train me. Our first session was set (as described in Chapter 2) and it was the beginning of some of the hardest

NELL'S MARATHON PROGRESS	
2004: 3 hr 22 min	2009: 3 hr 10 min
2005: 3 hr 10 min	2011: 3 hr 08 min
2007: 5 hr 33 min (ran with my mum)	2012: 2 hr 54 min

training I'd ever done. Once a week he had me doing sessions of shuttle runs, burpees and press-ups, along with boxing on pads and dragging a tyre attached by a rope around my waist. Jim was brilliant at pushing me to my limits and was so encouraging.

The hard work paid off and I felt fitter and faster. I did the same races in the build-up to London that I had done the year before and was encouraged when I ran both quicker. At Reading I ran just over 1 hour 27 minutes, and at the Spen 20 I ran 2 hours and 23 minutes. I went into London feeling confident, and I was elated when I achieved a PB by 22 minutes, crossing the line in 3 hours and 10 minutes. I couldn't believe I had run that fast. It meant I had qualified for a 'championship' place in the London Marathon the following year.

However I was then delighted to have my son, Devon, in 2006 so I obviously didn't run a marathon that year. In 2007, I agreed to do it with my mum, Nancy, and run at her pace. We finished in just over 5½ hours. It was a completely different experience for me to walk-run round without worrying about finishing in the fastest time I could manage. It also made me truly appreciate running a marathon is hard whatever your pace – I wasn't pushing myself to run hard, but I was on my feet for much longer and my stride was shorter, which is tiring in a different way. I had to keep encouraging my mum to keep going and I'm so proud of her for finishing. You can read her thoughts on the experience further on in this chapter – she did enjoy most of it!

Taking part made me want to run it again so I signed up for the following year. By then, Devon was two and I was still breastfeeding so I was having broken nights' sleep and wasn't able to fit in as much training as I would have liked.

I did the Reading Half and the Spen 20 again, this time in 1 hour 28 minutes, and 2 hours 22 minutes respectively. I had run similar times before having Devon so I felt a PB at London might not be possible, but I would still be able to finish and do

well. I didn't want to push myself to train harder at this time in case I got ill or injured. I had to be flexible about my training around caring for Devon, plus I wanted to spend more time with him than running as he was constantly changing and developing. I didn't want to miss out on those precious times, which I could never experience again, as I knew there would be other races when he was older. In the end, I finished in 3 hours and 10 minutes again, which I was satisfied with.

Two years later, I then knocked 2 minutes off to run 3 hours and 8 minutes, feeling comfortable most of the way. By now Devon was older and had started school. I knew I had a sub-three hour in me if I could just get the training in...

With my mum running the Cancer Research UK 10K at Harewood House, Leeds

HOW I RAN SUB-THREE

To run sub-three in 2012, I knew I would have to be more focused in the build-up to the race. I made 2 hours 59 minutes my goal, which would mean running at a pace of 6 minutes and 50 seconds per mile. That was 20 seconds per mile faster than I had run before.

I read the book *Marathon Running* by Richard Nerurkar for his tips. Richard is an accomplished GB athlete with a PB of 2 hours and 8 minutes. His many achievements include winning the Hamburg Marathon and finishing fifth in the marathon at the Atlanta Olympics, so he certainly knows his stuff. From the book I learnt that lifestyle habits, such as daily diet and average hours of sleep per night, are important components of a marathon-training plan. He also writes about the importance of holding something back for the last 6 miles – so you should treat 20 miles as being half way through the race. Up to that point, you should be controlling the pace and not try to go too fast. I devised a training plan based on the sub-three training regimes in his book (which he has kindly allowed me to reproduce – you can find the schedules at the back of the book, see pages 194–195). I aimed to follow the sub-2 hour 20 minute plan. I knew I wouldn't get anywhere near achieving that time but I thought if I could do similar mileage to what people of that standard do, I would be guaranteed to run faster. I was also aware that because I'm a mother, I would need to be flexible with my training. So if I couldn't follow the sub-2 hour 20 minute plan to the letter, I could fall back and do the sub-2 hour 45 minute schedule instead.

I also kept Googling sub-three marathon discussions to find out how other people had done it. I wanted to find out how I could get to 18 miles at that pace and not blow up. I kept reading that the best way to do it was to increase your mileage so your legs can handle it – so that's what I did. I knew it wouldn't be easy, but you can't just turn up and run a sub-three marathon, you have to put the work in. So for the 12-week build-up to the marathon, I was mostly just running, preparing and eating and being a mum to Devon – I didn't have a social life of any kind!

I wanted to get up to 80 to 90 miles a week. To fit this in, I would need to train twice a day around the school run. So most weekdays, I would run in the morning after dropping Devon off at school, go home, eat, do a bit of work and then be back running again at 2p.m. so I was then able to collect Devon from school at 3p.m.

Evenings would be spent getting Devon's tea, helping him do his homework and putting him to bed. Then I'd get an early night myself – a couple of times a week, as early as 8.30p.m.

On Tuesdays, I did intervals on my own off-road in Bushey Park such as 8 x 1k hard with 90 seconds' jog recovery. On a Thursday, I would run a fartlek with bursts of running faster for 20 minutes within a

run. I think these speed sessions made all the difference as they added variety to my training and improved my pace.

I did a mid-week run of 12–14 miles and my longest run at the weekend, building up the distance each week. That meant I did six 18–20 milers in the build-up plus a couple of 24-mile runs at the peak of the programme. In comparison, the first time I did the marathon, I only did one 20-mile run. I think those long runs meant my body could cope better on race day. I always did them at a steady speed, slower than my target marathon pace, so it didn't tire me out for the rest of the week's training.

Before the 12-week plan started, I had regularly been doing weights and strength training, which was important as it meant my body was strong before I started doing extra mileage. When I was doing 90 miles a week, I didn't have the time

or energy to do this kind of training so instead I did core stability exercises a few times a week and strengthening exercises occasionally, such as squats.

Aside from the 20-mile run at the weekend and one 12–14 mid-week run, most of my other runs were around 5–6 miles. I think this was how my body coped with the increase in training, as doing shorter runs was manageable and I was able to recover in between. Fitting in and doing 10 miles a day seemed a lot so splitting it into two 5-mile runs – one in the morning, one in the afternoon – made it feel easier.

Fitting the training in each week often required forward planning around work and family commitments. For example, if I had to have a meeting in central London, I would take my running gear in a backpack so I could run home instead of getting the train. On some weekends, I would have to get up and creep out for a run early in the morning before the rest of the family woke up. I would also have to be flexible and accept I wouldn't always be able to stick exactly to the schedule. It is important to have a plan but not to get too hung up on it. If you miss a session because you're too busy or too tired, then don't give up on the whole thing. You might need to reschedule the session for another day or take a rest day on a different day than originally intended. Remember, all is not lost if you can't follow a schedule exactly.

As well as being more dedicated to getting the miles in, I also became stricter about my diet, as explained in the Food For Fuel chapter. I ate less sugar and made sure I was having carbs before a run and quickly refuelling with protein afterwards. I also kept snacks such as fruit and nuts handy if I was out and about so I didn't have dips in energy. I didn't want to miss a run because I was hungry or hadn't recovered from the last one, so eating the right foods at the right times was crucial.

At the start of the 12 weeks, I had a few weeks where I felt like I wasn't improving. Then as the training went on I could feel I was getting fitter, but I wasn't sure exactly what shape I was in as I was always training on my own.

At around seven weeks in, I did an off-road race, the Vale Gallop 10k, and I felt really good and strong, finishing in a time of 40 minutes 44 seconds. It was a spur of the moment decision to do it and it really boosted my confidence and assured me the training plan was working.

I had two other races planned for March and I wanted to run those well and see how fast I could go. The first was the Bath Half in the second week of March. It was a two-lap course, which I wasn't sure about as I thought that could make it mentally tougher, but I really enjoyed it. The route is mostly flat and there's brilliant crowd support all the way. I ran a PB of 1 hour and 21 minutes and I was over the moon. It made me realise sub-three could be possible, but I had to keep ticking over in training.

A couple of weeks after Bath, I did the National Lottery Olympic Park five mile race. This was the first opportunity to see the London 2012 Olympic Park and runners would finish inside the athletics stadium, so it was an opportunity I couldn't turn down. The course had lots of twists and turns, but I still managed to run at a decent pace and loved having a sprint finish on the athletics track feeling like an Olympian. I ran a PB of 29 minutes 21 seconds and was amazed to learn I was the first woman to finish. It was another confidence boost ahead of the

MY RACES IN 2012

Vale Gallop 10K trail race
Sunday 26th February
Finishing time: 40.44.

Bath Half
Sunday 11th March
Finishing time: 81.51.

National Lottery Olympic Parkrun (5 miles)
Sunday 31st March
Finishing time: 29.21.

London Marathon
Sunday 22nd April
Finishing time: 2.54.39.

marathon which was now a month away.

With three weeks to go till the race, I did my longest run. It ended up being 24 miles in total, but it was a bit stop and start. I'd been in London for the Sport Relief Mile so after I had run that at an easy pace, I then ran home to West London. I set off jogging and kept it steady and had occasional stops to have sips of water. It wasn't super fast, but was just about time on my feet.

After this long run, I started tapering and for the next three weeks I did fewer runs so my weekly mileage decreased to about 70, then 50 miles. In the final week before the race, I either did easy-to-steady five mile runs or rested.

Even though I was running a lot less, that last week of the 12 week plan leading up to the marathon was the worst! I constantly felt physically sick and so nervous. I just kept hoping things would go well on race day after all the training and sacrifices. I wanted to make all those runs in the cold and the rain worth it.

The day of the race arrived and I tried to put my nerves to one side and be confident. I knew I had put in the miles and the hard work, I just had to go for it.

Thanks to my finishing time the year before, I had qualified to be on the championship 'blue' start. This was an unknown for me as I'd previously always been on the 'green' start with the celebrity runners. The women on the championship start were all high-standard club runners capable of a sub-3 hour 15 minute marathon or sub-90 minute half marathons. They all looked really fast so it felt more serious than on the celeb start.

I was watching what everyone else was doing to prepare, what they had for breakfast, what shoes they wore, how much they drank. I wanted to go round and ask them all about their training as I was fascinated! But I had to focus instead on my own race so I took my extra layers off, handed my bag into the baggage truck and headed to the start line where I lined up behind the elite men and speedy club runners.

After they announced the men in the elite field to rounds of applause, the gun went and we were off. I felt really good and I went through the first mile in just over 6 minutes. I knew this was too fast so I pulled it back. Even though that pace had felt easy, I knew if I carried on like that I could hit the wall at mile 18 and regret it. So the next few miles I ran at 6 minute 30 seconds pace. It was faster than I needed to run for 2 hours 59 minutes, but I felt comfortable so I thought I would stick with it. I kept it up till half way, going through that point in 1 hour 25 minutes.

I started crying as I reached Buckingham Palace

At mile 15, I thought 'I'm flying here, I feel great'. But by 20 miles it was getting harder and my pace started slipping. However, I knew if I could just hold on and not slow too much, I could still get sub-three.

In the last few miles I tried to ignore the fatigue in my legs and pretended I was just out for my usual 4-mile run. I tried to visualise how I felt on those short runs to help me get to the finish.

Finally, I passed Buckingham Palace and coming down The Mall I could see the finish line and the clock showing I was well inside 3 hours. I couldn't believe it. I strode for the line with a big smile on my face finishing in 2 hours 54 minutes and 39 seconds. I had done it! I felt so emotional – proud, exhausted, relieved, ecstatic – I burst into tears. By the time I got my medal I couldn't stop smiling. I was on such a high.

Then it was back to reality – home on the Tube, then making the Sunday dinner and doing the washing up! But for the rest of the week I was on cloud nine, I still couldn't believe I had run sub-three. All the hard work had paid off. I proudly put my sticker showing my finishing time on our fridge and it's still there today – reminding me of what I can do when I put my mind to it, and inspiring me to get back into that shape again.

After London, I took some time off running to let my body recover from the marathon. I didn't do anything for a week. Then, when I resumed running, I did less mileage and more strength and conditioning work at Locker 27 (locker27.com). It was great to do some different exercises after the marathon training and I loved doing things like box jumps and pull-ups. Locker 27 advocate using weights to enhance your athletic ability and this is something I have found works for me. I was still the

Completing such a huge challenge can be really emotional

fittest I had ever been after the London Marathon, despite no longer doing 90 miles a week. To make the most of it, I thought I would try reducing my 10k time as I didn't want to do another long-distance race. I did the Bupa Great Manchester Run and achieved a PB of 36 minutes 54 seconds six weeks after London. It's a race with a great atmosphere and it felt good to stop at 6 miles instead of carrying on for another 20! I think switching to strength and conditioning exercises, speed work and less mileage helped me combat losing motivation following the marathon.

After that, I was delighted to become pregnant with Anya, so running marathons hasn't been on the agenda in recent years. But I'm still not done with marathon running. Having achieved sub-three feeling comfortable for most of the way, I now believe I could go even faster. I know it will take more hard work and training, but I'd love to break 2 hours 45 minutes – that would be unbelievable. But it won't be until I can dedicate myself to the training when the children are older. So watch this space...!

MY SUB-THREE MARATHON PROGRAMME

Here's the training I did on a typical week in the build-up to my 2012 London Marathon. If you do use a similar format, remember I followed this schedule after running a 3 hour 8 minute marathon and was in reasonable state of fitness. So this programme is not recommended for beginners but for those who are already used to running at least 50 miles a week.

DAY	AM	PM
1	6 miles easy	6 miles steady
2	4–6 miles easy	2-mile warm-up jog, interval session, e.g. 8 x 1K with 90-second recovery, or 3 x 3k with a 3 minute recovery, 2-mile warm-down jog
3	Long run, easy-to-steady building up miles, then tapering – so weeks one to four I ran 12 miles, weeks five to 10 I ran 14 miles, then in weeks 11 and 12 I ran 5 miles	
4	6 miles easy	8 miles with 20 minutes' fartlek
5	5 miles steady	6 miles easy but including 20 x 30-second strides
6	Rest day at the beginning (weeks one to four) and end (weeks 10–12) of the programme, but in weeks five to nine I did an easy run of 4–6 miles	
7	Longest run, easy-to-steady pace, building up each week to 24 miles. After that, in the two Sundays before the marathon, I did 14 miles then 12 miles	

NOTE

My 'easy' pace was around 8-minute miling, 'steady' was around 7-minute miling, and intervals and fartlek efforts at around 6-minute miling.

Find more detailed marathon training plans at the back of the book.

MARATHONERS' STORIES

Training for, and running, a marathon is a real experience and a steep learning curve. I love hearing about other people's marathon journeys – what worked for them and what they learnt about themselves in the process. Here's a selection of stories from a variety of motivated and inspirational runners...

THE SUB-7-HOUR RUNNERS...

'The atmosphere was like one big street party'

In Chapter 4, **Abi Wright** revealed how she changed her diet, took up running and lost a massive 14st. She then set herself the challenge of running a marathon, here she recounts how she found the experience...

'When I was at my biggest, the London Marathon was never an option so being able to take part was very special to me. I wasn't aiming to finish in a certain time, just getting round was enough of a target.

'I found Twitter was a great motivational tool as I shared my training with other people and was overwhelmed by the support I received from people I had never met.

'As soon as the race started I felt amazing. I couldn't believe I was actually a part of the London Marathon. The first couple of miles flew by, however when we got to 3 miles a niggling back issue I'd had in the build-up kicked in. I knew I only had one choice and that was to grit my teeth and fight through it. Despite the pain, I was still enjoying the experience, running alongside other people who were also battling for the 26.2 was inspiring.

'When we ran over Tower Bridge I could hear my family roar me on.

'My worst mile was at 15 when I started crying like a baby as I was worried about how I was going to finish when there was still such a long way to go. Allan advised me to focus on reaching small targets such as the next water station, rather than thinking about the finish line. It worked and in no time at all we were at mile 22.

'The final few miles were tough, but the atmosphere was like one big street party which helped keep me going. By mile 25, my body was in a lot of pain, my back was screaming and my feet were burning – I had expected running a marathon to hurt, but I'd never felt anything like it. But when the finish line appeared, everything seemed worth it. I finished in 6 hours 47 minutes and broke down in tears of joy (and exhaustion!). I was delighted to get my medal, and then met my friends and family for an emotional celebration. I couldn't have done it without their support.

'My legs were sore for days after the race, but it was worth it. Sunday 13th April 2014 was the best day of my life so far.'

Follow Abi on Twitter@ abiwrightoni

'It's unlikely I'll experience that level of euphoria crossing a finish line again'

Jamie Singer, from Oxford, has run seven marathons and has a PB of 4 hours 32 minutes. But he cites his first marathon in London – in which he ran his slowest time in utter agony – as his favourite. Here's why...

'When training for my first London Marathon in 2008, I was diagnosed with runner's knee – apparently it's very common and easy to fix (see the injury section earlier in the book, page 83). But I didn't find time to do the physio exercises so it didn't improve.

'My physio assured me I would still be able to race without doing any permanent damage so I decided to go ahead.

'On the day, I made the mistake of drinking three large bottles of water before the start. This meant by mile 3, I was desperate for the toilet and had to queue for the on-course loos. When I emerged, I saw the horror that is the sweep coach (which crawls around the back of the field picking up injured athletes) appear on the brow of the hill. There may not be any greater feeling of despair in a race of 35,000 athletes than realising you are at the very back of the field. I attempted to make up some time by running faster than I had originally intended. This was another error – by mile 6, my knee was in a lot of pain.

'Crossing Tower Bridge almost by myself was not the marathon experience I had dreamed of, but I was amazed by the many supporters who had stayed out to cheer me on in the pouring rain.

'I finally turned the corner into The Mall and the sight of the finish was magical.

'I haven't got a word to describe the feeling of finishing something that you've dreamt of doing your entire life – it is something you have to experience for yourself. My time of 6 hours 42 minutes may not have been the fastest, but I had a shiny medal around my neck, and that was all that really mattered.

'As a result of listening to my physio, training hard but sensibly and not overindulging in water before the start, in 2013 I ran my seventh marathon and gained a PB of 4 hours 32 minutes.

'I've enjoyed and endured each of the marathons since my first, but it was my painful induction that I often cite as my favourite experience. Pushing myself to do something when it would have been easier to quit, feeling the generosity of the crowd and achieving a life-long dream to complete the London Marathon – it's unlikely I'll ever experience that level of euphoria at crossing the line again.'

Follow Jamie on Twitter @jamjsin.

THE SUB-6-HOUR RUNNERS...

'I should have listened to my daughter and done more training!'

I persuaded my mum, **Nancy McAndrew**, to run the marathon in 2007 and I ran round the whole way with her. Here's how she found it...

'I ran the London Marathon in 2007 partly as a way of getting fitter, but also to prove to myself that, at the age of 54, I was capable and dedicated enough to do something as amazing as running 26.2 miles. Raising money for charity was an added bonus.

'Leading up to the marathon, I started training three to four days a week, trying to fit in some long-distance runs, speed and hill running with lots of support and advice from my daughter.

'At the time, I felt I was putting in plenty of training, but looking back it was nowhere near enough and my daughter regularly reminded me that I should be putting much more effort into my training or I would live to regret it, or even suffer an injury.

'On the day of the marathon, the best bits were the incredible atmosphere, the fantastic support from the crowds and completing it in a time of 5 hours 35 minutes.

'The worst bits were the overpowering nausea I experienced during the last 10 miles or so and when I finally finished, being hopelessly unable to put one foot in front of the other or bend my legs at all! Eventually, I had to be helped into my grandson's buggy and pushed through some very smart areas of London to our hotel. When I was finally helped on to a bed and my blood-soaked socks removed, my feet were covered in blisters and I had lost a couple of toenails.

'Would I do it again? Yes, but I would certainly take my daughter's advice more seriously and do far more training than I did first time round! I know I couldn't have done it without her and at no point would she leave me to continue on my own, even though I know it was much harder for her to run at my pace and she would have probably finished a good few hours earlier had she run the marathon at her own speed.

'Writing this has brought back all those memories of exhaustion, happiness and pride at what we all can achieve with a bit of hard work and lots of dedication.

'I'm pretty undecided on whether I actually enjoyed the experience'

Dean Piper is a showbiz writer for the national press so when he swapped rubbing shoulders with celebrities for pounding the pavements marathon training, he didn't quite know what he had let himself in for...

'I was never one of those natural runners. You know, the ones who seem to continually stampede past you in the park.

'But after 'competing' in two triathlons and raising £10,000 for Macmillan Cancer Support, I decided to up my game. The marathon always seemed out of reach for me and I wanted to prove I could do it.

'Everything I did revolved around the marathon and as the day got closer I had so many questions. Had I done enough training? Was I going to get sore nipples? What if I needed a number two as I was running?

'In the end I had to chill out and hope for the best. I set myself a target of 4 hours and 30 minutes which seemed achievable based on my training times.

'On the big day I was feeling good, the sun was out, and I was running, once again, for the fantastic Macmillan Cancer Support.

'The first 7 miles were a dream and up until half way I loved it. But from Tower Bridge it was hell.

'After the bridge, the course doubles back. Psychologically it was gutting to see the super-fast runners who had reached the 20-mile mark zooming past when I was only at 14 miles.

'From Canary Wharf I was close to tears, my legs were seizing up and my nipples were raw. I was getting slower and the time I wanted to achieve was sliding away.

'By the time I got to 23 miles I was having to walk and people in the crowd kept shouting at me to keep running which was driving me mad. One had a sign saying: "Only 5 miles to go!" – I felt like whacking them. Five miles after running 21 is such hard work! I decided to walk it out and enjoy the final bit... no matter how slow I was.

'I ended up crossing the line in 5 hours and 35 minutes. It was over an hour slower than the time I had wanted to achieve – but I FINISHED A MARATHON.

'So you get the picture, it wasn't the easiest experience – but honesty is the name of the marathon game. Be honest with what your body can achieve.

'Unlike most people who run a marathon, I remain pretty undecided on whether I actually enjoyed the experience. If I did it again I'd train far more and get my long runs up to 21 miles (the longest I did was 19).

'I occasionally look at my medal with a smirk of achievement and ponder running it again. Then I remember the guy dressed as Big Bird who overtook me with 600m to go – and go back to ordering a takeaway!'

Follow Dean on Twitter @deanpiper.

THE SUB-4-HOUR RUNNERS...

'Despite how painful it was, there was no way I wasn't going to finish'

Journalist **Rosie Millard**, 48, from Islington, has four children and has run a number of marathons, including a particularly gruelling one along the Great Wall of China.

'I was asked to run the London Marathon in 2008 with my husband, Philip, and write about our experience in *The Times*.

'Wanting to run the marathon and actually doing it are two very different things and I embarked on the training with a sense of dread. It wasn't just the fact it was 26.2 miles long, but that I would have to run surrounded by people. I'm usually a lone runner. I like to run without a watch or listening to music as it's my time to think about work and my children. I couldn't imagine how I would cope running for that long surrounded by noise, spectators, and thousands of other runners.

'In preparation, I entered a number of races to get me used to the race environment. I also prepared mental strategies like breaking the race up into sections to make it seem more manageable.

'During the marathon, when it got hard, I thought of the charity I was raising money for and remembered all the exhausting long runs I had put in over the winter.

'I finished in 3 hours and 51 minutes. Crossing the finish line can only be summed up as a great life moment.

'I vowed I would never run another marathon, but of course I quickly changed my mind. Marathon running is addictive and now I want to do the six World Marathon Majors – London, Berlin, Boston,

Chicago, New York and Tokyo.

'I'm now two down and four to go having recently ticked Berlin off the list. I ran it in 2013, beating my London time by 20 seconds, even though I hadn't trained as hard as I would have liked. I think the key difference was that I had undertaken more speed work.

'My greatest challenge was completing the Great Wall of China Marathon. The route involves conquering 5,164 steps with some sections alongside a terrifying 100ft drop. Despite how painful it got, there was no way I wasn't going to finish and I did so in 5 hours and 41 minutes. It didn't matter that it wasn't a PB time, finishing was the achievement.'

Follow Rosie on Twitter @rosiemillard and read her blog at http://rosiemillard1.wordpress.com/

'Running the marathon was part of my journey to overcome cancer'

I've had the pleasure of meeting **Findlay Young**, 41, through racing for Cancer Research UK. Here, he shares his incredible and inspiring story of how he continued to run and race while battling cancer...

'At school I was probably the least likely to run, but I got the running bug in my twenties. I was keen to improve and wanted to get under 3 hour 30 minutes, so I made this my target when I entered the Chicago Marathon in 2003. But then cancer stopped everything.

'When I was first diagnosed with thyroid cancer it hit me pretty hard. People suddenly wanted to constantly check how I was – in reality I just wanted to get back to "normal". Running was my way of keeping things the way they were before my diagnosis.

'I abruptly found myself in a hospital bed having radiotherapy and then subsequent operations – all I wanted to was to do was go for a run. I remember one day putting my trainers on and then just sitting on the sofa. I had no physical energy to run, but in my head I still wanted to go.

'I managed a few runs between treatments and eventually on 26th September I was told I no longer had cancer, and so on 10th October I committed to running the marathon and raising money for Cancer Research UK.

'Standing on the start line, still with a dressing covering my recent surgery, was an incredible moment – I had made it, no matter what had happened.

'The support on the course was amazing. For the first time when running a marathon, I didn't have any low points. One word – cancer – kept me going. The part I remember most is getting to the finish line, seeing my friends and knowing this was part of my journey to overcome the disease. Two weeks after surgery, I was happy to finish in a time of 3 hours and 39 minutes. It was just 9 minutes off my original target despite all I had been through.

'Since then, I have had cancer twice again and had over 48 lots of treatment. At the same time, I continued to complete challenges including running four half marathons in 24 hours, and 24 half marathons in 24 time zones, on 24 consecutive days (Great World Run), raising more than £100k.

'In 2015 I will be running 2,015k, starting with 48 runs in 12 days ahead of the London Marathon. Cancer is no longer part of me but running still is. It keeps me calm, gives me a focus and I just love it.'

Follow Findlay on Twitter @run2015km.

174

'I've learnt something new every time I've raced the marathon'

My co-writer, **Lucy**, has had various ups and downs as she's run the London Marathon four times. Here she reveals what she's learnt along the way...

'Before 2009, I had mostly raced over shorter distances up to 5k with the occasional 10k and one half marathon under my belt, so covering 26.2 miles was a daunting prospect.

'I increased my long runs each week until I eventually ran 20 miles. However, other than that, I didn't increase my training and I didn't pay much attention to my diet. I thought carb-loading just meant having a big bowl of pasta the night before the race.

'On the day, I made the classic mistake of going off too fast thanks to the fantastic atmosphere and the downhill start. My target pace (I was aiming for sub-3 hours 15 minutes) felt easy so I decided to make the most of feeling good by going faster, believing that if I then hit the wall I would still finish on target if I then slowed down. I hadn't realised that when hitting the wall I wouldn't slow by seconds per mile but by minutes.

'Those last 6 miles were hell. It was a warm day and I hadn't drunk enough so I became dehydrated. By mile 22, I felt dizzy and light-headed and my calves were cramping up. I struggled to finish, disappointed with my time of 3 hours and 19 minutes. After the race I couldn't move without pain for a week, but I was determined to do the marathon again.

'The following year I improved by 2 minutes but again struggled in the last 6 miles. In 2011 I had a breakthrough – finishing in 3 hours and 6 minutes.

By then, I had learnt to start taking on carbs the Wednesday before the race and had practised taking energy gels in training.

'I started conservatively, checking my Garmin constantly and easing back if I went too fast. Instead of hating those final 6 miles, I loved them. I felt strong all the way to the finish line – something I had previously never imagined was possible.

'In 2012, I made it my target to run sub-three but despite a good build-up – including running a half marathon PB of 1 hour and 23 minutes – it was not meant to be. I caught an infection in the week before the race and had to take antibiotics. My doctor said I would be ok to run but wouldn't be at my best. I ran 3 hours and 6 minutes again and it felt like a missed opportunity.

'In 2013, a busy workload meant I couldn't fit in the training and in 2014, my plans to race were ruined by a foot injury. So I remain determined to run sub-three one day – which gives me great motivation to keep training.'

Follow Lucy on Twitter @LucyRunningFeat

THE SUB-3-HOUR RUNNERS...

'I couldn't believe the clock when I crossed the finish line'

June Allen, 40, from Essex, has run some fantastic marathon times – including a PB of 2 hours and 46 minutes, despite having to fit her training in around a challenging full-time job as an assistant headteacher. Here, she reveals how she improved and how she overcame one particularly horrendous race experience during which she ended up in hospital...

'I took up running for the 2006 London Marathon and hoped to finish in around 4 hours – which I did with 2 minutes to spare. I was over the moon and had thoroughly enjoyed the race.

'It gave me the running bug and I ran a 10-mile race in the May, where I started talking to people from my local running club – Springfield Striders – and they encouraged me to join.

'I kept improving, but then I started to get knee issues and ended up having surgery. I worried I would never run again but the operation worked and my knee now seems as good as new.

'In 2011, I was ready to run the London Marathon again. Training went well until I picked up a slight injury ahead of the race. I didn't want to miss the race so I took some painkillers before the start to get me through. However, I didn't realise one of the side effects of the painkillers was dehydration. This led to disaster at mile 21 when I collapsed and was taken to hospital. I lost my memory for hours and was attached to a drip. When I eventually came round, I was not in a good way. Stupidly, I hadn't written my personal details on my number so my family were unaware of what had happened.

'It was a scary experience and left me not wanting to run another marathon ever again.

'However, I finally decided to give it a shot the following year, going for sub-three. This time, everything went to plan. I felt great all of the way round and came in just after Nell in 2 hours 55 minutes. I was delighted, especially as I had done it after the horrible experience the previous year.

'I had a lovely chat with Nell, we hit it off straight away as we are both passionate about running. She was amazed I fit my training in around a full-time job as an assistant headteacher. I manage twice-a-day training by getting up at 5a.m. for my first run of the day and I do my second training session after work, sometimes as late as 9p.m. if I've had a parents' evening.

'In 2013 I did the Manchester Marathon and could not believe the clock when I crossed the finish line in 2 hours 46 minutes.

'It hasn't always been plain sailing for me so big things I have learnt include not to run a marathon unless you are 100 per cent well. Don't go off too fast, take on plenty of fluid and always write your contact details on the back of your running number. And lastly – enjoy it!'

'Lining up next to Olympic and World champions was quite nerve-wracking!'

Lucy's sister, **AMY WHITEHEAD**, 36, is an elite marathon runner with a PB of 2 hours 33 minutes. At the 2014 London Marathon, she lined up on the elite women's start with the aim of qualifying for the Commonwealth Games. Here, she reveals what it's like to start a marathon alongside the world's best long-distance runners with a place in a major championship at stake...

'After three years running on the mass start of the London Marathon and getting faster each time, I was invited to join the women's elite field in 2012 – which sets off 45 minutes ahead of the masses.

'There was a strong group of Brits vying for selection for the Olympics and although I ran a PB of 2 hours 33 minutes, it wasn't fast enough to qualify. Then in 2013, Susan Partridge and I were the only Brits in the elite field aiming to qualify for the World Championships. I was in good shape, but a fast start hanging off the back of some of the world's best runners meant I faded towards the end and again missed the qualifying time.

'I was disappointed and wondered if I should give up trying to achieve an England vest. But with the Commonwealth Games in Glasgow the following summer, my family, coach George Gandy and friend and advisor, Liz Yelling, encouraged me to keep going. Thanks to their support, and that of my physio Mark Buckingham, I lined up in my sixth London Marathon determined to be selected for the Commonwealths.

'The Saturday before the race, all the elite athletes are put up in the Tower Hotel by Tower Bridge. The atmosphere is fairly relaxed. At the same time, you are aware you are part of something big.

'On the morning of the race, I got up at 5.30a.m. with my ever-supportive and calm husband Andy, and had my usual pre-marathon meal – three slices of toast (brown bread) with jam. This tops up my carb stores after carbo-loading for the previous few days.

'Once at the start, there's a separate tent for the elite athletes. It's quite different to being on the mass start, which feels like a party in some ways. The elite tent is calm and quiet with everyone focused on their own pre-race routine.

'When the race started, the Olympians sped off, but I was under strict instructions from my coach to run cautiously and not risk blowing up.

'This meant I spent the majority of the race without another athlete in sight. Having run on the mass start, it's a strange experience to run with the course completely to yourself and it can be mentally tough to keep going. But the crowds are amazing and the bonus of being the only runner on the road is they are all cheering for you! Their support really drove me to keep working hard.

'In the end I ran near perfect splits to finish first Brit with the qualifying time. Next stop the Commonwealth Games!'

Follow Amy on Twitter @AmyRunningFeat.

USEFUL INFORMATION

In the remaining pages you will find a pace chart to help you when training and racing, training schedules kindly provided by Sensev El-Ahmadi, Alan Dent and Richard Nerurkar, addresses for useful running-related websites and recommended reading.

The pace chart on the following page will help you work out what your race pace is so you can practise it in training. For example, if you are aiming for a marathon in 4 hours, your marathon pace is 9.10 so you should run at this pace in marathon pace training runs and stick to this pace from the start of the race. You can also use the chart to help you predict what you might be capable of in a longer race based on your previous race times for 5k/10k/ half marathon. If you have run a 2 hour half marathon (9.10 pace), your pace will be at least 20 seconds per mile slower (9.30) making your target marathon time 4hr 8 min 54 sec.

Another tip: if you are aiming, for example, for a 4 hour marathon, memorise the 5k, 10k, half marathon and 20 mile splits to ensure you are on track during the race.

RUNNING PACE CHART

Mile pace	5K	5 Miles	10K	15K	10 Miles	20K
05:00	15:32	25:00	31:04	46:36	50:00	01:02:08
05:30	17:05	27:30	34:11	51:16	55:00	01:08:21
06:00	18:38	30:00	37:17	55:55	01:00:00	01:14:34
06:10	19:10	30:50	38:19	57:29	01:01:40	01:16:38
06:20	19:41	31:40	39:21	59:02	01:03:20	01:18:42
06:30	20:12	32:30	40:23	01:00:35	01:05:00	01:20:47
06:40	20:43	33:20	41:25	01:02:08	01:06:40	01:22:51
06:50	21:14	34:10	42:28	01:03:41	01:08:20	01:24:55
07:00	21:45	35:00	43:30	01:05:15	01:10:00	01:27:00
07:10	22:16	35:50	44:32	01:06:48	01:11:40	01:29:04
07:20	22:47	36:40	45:34	01:08:21	01:13:20	01:31:08
07:30	23:18	37:30	46:36	01:09:54	01:15:00	01:33:12
07:40	23:49	38:20	47:38	01:11:27	01:16:40	01:35:17
07:50	24:20	39:10	48:40	01:13:01	01:18:20	01:37:21
08:00	24:51	40:00	49:43	01:14:34	01:20:00	01:39:25
08:10	25:22	40:50	50:45	01:16:07	01:21:40	01:41:29
08:20	25:53	41:40	51:47	01:17:40	01:23:20	01:43:34
08:30	26:24	42:30	52:49	01:19:13	01:25:00	01:45:38
08:40	26:56	43:20	53:51	01:20:47	01:26:40	01:47:42
08:50	27:27	44:10	54:53	01:22:20	01:28:20	01:49:47
09:00	27:58	45:00	55:55	01:23:53	01:30:00	01:51:51
09:10	28:29	45:50	56:58	01:25:26	01:31:40	01:53:55
09:20	29:00	46:40	58:00	01:27:00	01:33:20	01:55:59
09:30	29:31	47:30	59:02	01:28:33	01:35:00	01:58:04
09:40	30:02	48:20	01:00:04	01:30:06	01:36:40	02:00:08
09:50	30:33	49:10	01:01:06	01:31:39	01:38:20	02:02:12
10:00	31:04	50:00	01:02:08	01:33:12	01:40:00	02:04:16
10:10	31:35	50:50	01:03:10	01:34:46	01:41:40	02:06:21
10:20	32:06	51:40	01:04:13	01:36:19	01:43:20	02:08:25
10:30	32:37	52:30	01:05:15	01:37:52	01:45:00	02:10:29
10:40	33:08	53:20	01:06:17	01:39:25	01:46:40	02:12:34
10:50	33:39	54:10	01:07:19	01:40:58	01:48:20	02:14:38
11:00	34:11	55:00	01:08:21	01:42:32	01:50:00	02:16:42
11:10	34:42	55:50	01:09:23	01:44:05	01:51:40	02:18:46
11:20	35:13	56:40	01:10:25	01:45:38	01:53:20	02:20:51
11:30	35:44	57:30	01:11:27	01:47:11	01:55:00	02:22:55
11:40	36:15	58:20	01:12:30	01:48:44	01:56:40	02:24:59
11:50	36:46	59:10	01:13:32	01:50:18	01:58:20	02:27:03
12:00	37:17	1:00:00	01:14:34	01:51:51	02:00:00	02:29:08

Half Marathon	15 Miles	25K	30K	20 Miles	35K	40K	Marathon
01:05:30	01:15:00	01:17:40	01:33:12	01:40:00	01:48:44	02:04:16	02:11:00
01:12:03	01:22:30	01:25:26	01:42:32	01:50:00	01:59:37	02:16:42	02:24:06
01:18:36	01:30:00	01:33:12	01:51:51	02:00:00	02:10:29	02:29:08	02:37:12
01:20:47	01:32:30	01:35:48	01:54:57	02:03:20	02:14:07	02:33:16	02:41:34
01:22:58	01:35:00	01:38:23	01:58:04	02:06:40	02:17:44	02:37:25	02:45:56
01:25:09	01:37:30	01:40:58	02:01:10	02:10:00	02:21:22	02:41:33	02:50:18
01:27:20	01:40:00	01:43:34	02:04:16	02:13:20	02:24:59	02:45:42	02:54:40
01:29:31	01:42:30	01:46:09	02:07:23	02:16:40	02:28:37	02:49:50	02:59:02
01:31:42	01:45:00	01:48:44	02:10:29	02:20:00	02:32:14	02:53:59	03:03:24
01:33:53	01:47:30	01:51:20	02:13:36	02:23:20	02:35:52	02:58:08	03:07:46
01:36:04	01:50:00	01:53:55	02:16:42	02:26:40	02:39:29	03:02:16	03:12:08
01:38:15	01:52:30	01:56:30	02:19:49	02:30:00	02:43:07	03:06:25	03:16:30
01:40:26	01:55:00	01:59:06	02:22:55	02:33:20	02:46:44	03:10:33	03:20:52
01:42:37	01:57:30	02:01:41	02:26:01	02:36:40	02:50:22	03:14:42	03:25:14
01:44:48	02:00:00	02:04:16	02:29:08	02:40:00	02:53:59	03:18:50	03:29:36
01:46:59	02:02:30	02:06:52	02:32:14	02:43:20	02:57:37	03:22:59	03:33:58
01:49:10	02:05:00	02:09:27	02:35:21	02:46:40	03:01:14	03:27:07	03:38:20
01:51:21	02:07:30	02:12:02	02:38:27	02:50:00	03:04:51	03:31:16	03:42:42
01:53:32	02:10:00	02:14:38	02:41:33	02:53:20	03:08:29	03:35:25	03:47:04
01:55:43	02:12:30	02:17:13	02:44:40	02:56:40	03:12:06	03:39:33	03:51:26
01:57:54	02:15:00	02:19:49	02:47:46	03:00:00	03:15:44	03:43:42	03:55:48
02:00:05	02:17:30	02:22:24	02:50:53	03:03:20	03:19:21	03:47:50	04:00:10
02:02:16	02:20:00	02:24:59	02:53:59	03:06:40	03:22:59	03:51:59	04:04:32
02:04:27	02:22:30	02:27:35	02:57:05	03:10:00	03:26:36	03:56:07	04:08:54
02:06:38	02:25:00	02:30:10	03:00:12	03:13:20	03:30:14	04:00:16	04:13:16
02:08:49	02:27:30	02:32:45	03:03:18	03:16:40	03:33:51	04:04:24	04:17:38
02:11:00	02:30:00	02:35:21	03:06:25	03:20:00	03:37:29	04:08:33	04:22:00
02:13:11	02:32:30	02:37:56	03:09:31	03:23:20	03:41:06	04:12:41	04:26:22
02:15:22	02:35:00	02:40:31	03:12:38	03:26:40	03:44:44	04:16:50	04:30:44
02:17:33	02:37:30	02:43:07	03:15:44	03:30:00	03:48:21	04:20:59	04:35:06
02:19:44	02:40:00	02:45:42	03:18:50	03:33:20	03:51:59	04:25:07	04:39:28
02:21:55	02:42:30	02:48:17	03:21:57	03:36:40	03:55:36	04:29:16	04:43:50
02:24:06	02:45:00	02:50:53	03:25:03	03:40:00	03:59:14	04:33:24	04:48:12
02:26:17	02:47:30	02:53:28	03:28:10	03:43:20	04:02:51	04:37:33	04:52:34
02:28:28	02:50:00	02:56:03	03:31:16	03:46:40	04:06:29	04:41:41	04:56:56
02:30:39	02:52:30	02:58:39	03:34:22	03:50:00	04:10:06	04:45:50	05:01:18
02:32:50	02:55:00	03:01:14	03:37:29	03:53:20	04:13:44	04:49:58	05:05:40
02:35:01	02:57:30	03:03:49	03:40:35	03:56:40	04:17:21	04:54:07	05:10:02
02:37:12	03:00:00	03:06:25	03:43:42	04:00:00	04:20:59	04:58:15	05:14:24

RUNNING SCHEDULES

On the next few pages you will find beginners 5k and 10k plans courtesy of Sensev El-Ahmadi. For more information, please visit How We Run Club http://www.hwrc.me.uk

   If you have never run before, start with the 'Couch to 5k' plan in Chapter 1 and then progress to the plan overleaf. If you already have a fitness base (i.e. you can run continuously for 20 minutes), start with this plan when targeting your first 5k race.

BEGINNERS' 5K PLAN ▶

BY SENSEV EL-AHMADI

DAY / WEEK

	1	2	3	4	5	6	7	
	Rest Day	**EASY RUN** Run, easy pace, 20 mins • Cool down, 5 to 10 mins • Stretch	Rest Day	**EASY RUN** Run, easy pace, 20 mins • Cool down, 5 to 10 mins • Stretch	Rest day	Rest day	**EASY RUN** Run, easy pace, 20 mins • Cool down, 5 to 10 mins • Stretch	1
	Rest Day	**INTERVALS** Warm up, 15 mins • Run, threshold pace, 3 mins. Recovery run, 90 seconds. Repeat 5 times • Cool down, 5 to 10 mins • Stretch	Rest day	**THRESHOLD RUN** Run, easy pace, 5 minutes • Run, steady pace, 5 mins • Run, threshold pace, 5 mins • Run, easy pace, 5 mins • Cool down, 5 to 10 mins • Stretch	Rest day	Rest Day	**EASY RUN** Run, easy pace, 40 mins • Cool down, 5 to 10 mins • Stretch	2
	Rest Day	**INTERVALS** Warm up, 15 mins • Run, threshold pace, 5 mins. Recovery run, 2 mins. Repeat 3 times • Cool down, 5 to 10 mins • Stretch	Rest Day	**THRESHOLD RUN** Run, easy pace, 6 mins • Run, steady pace, 6 mins • Run, threshold pace, 6 mins • Run, easy pace, 6 mins • Cool down, 5 to 10 mins • Stretch	Rest day	Rest Day	**EASY RUN** Run, easy pace, 50 mins • Cool down, 5 to 10 mins • Stretch	3
	Rest Day	**INTERVAL** Warm up, 15 mins • Run, threshold pace, 6 mins. Recovery run, 2 mins. Repeat 3 times • Cool down, 5 to 10 mins. Stretch	Rest day	**THRESHOLD RUN** Run, easy pace, 8 mins • Run, steady pace, 8 mins • Run, threshold pace, 8 mins • Run, easy pace, 8 mins • Cool down, 5 to 10 mins • Stretch	Rest day	Rest Day	**EASY RUN** Run, easy pace, 60 mins • Cool down, 5 to 10 mins • Stretch	4
	Rest Day	**INTERVALS** Warm up, 15 mins • Run, threshold pace, 5 mins. Recovery run, 2 mins. Repeat 4 times • Cool down, 5 to 10 mins • Stretch	Rest day	**STEADY RUN** Run, easy pace, 10 mins • Run, steady pace, 10 mins • Run, easy pace, 10 mins • Cool down, 5 to 10 mins • Stretch	Rest day	Rest Day	**EASY RUN** Run, easy pace, 30 mins • Cool down, 5 to 10 mins • Stretch • Cool down, 5 to 10 mins • Stretch	5
	Rest Day	**INTERVALS** Warm up, 15 mins • Run, threshold pace, 5 minutes. Recovery run, 2 mins. Repeat 3 times • Cool down, 5 to 10 mins • Stretch	Rest day	**EASY RUN** Run, easy pace, 20 mins • Cool down, 5 to 10 mins • Stretch	Rest day	**RECOVERY RUN** Run, easy pace, 10 mins • Cool down, 5 to 10 mins • Stretch	**5k Race**	6

NOTES

For a definition of intervals and threshold runs see pages 41–44.

BEGINNERS' 10K PLAN

BY SENSEV EL-AHMADI

If you have never run before and are targeting your first 10k race, start at week one. If you have a little more experience, e.g. you have trained for and raced a 5k, start at week 7. For definitions of intervals, threshold and fartlek, see pages 41–44

WEEK \ DAY	1	2	3	4	5	6	7
1	Rest Day	**INTERVALS** Run, easy pace, 5 mins. Brisk walk, 5 mins. Repeat 2 times • Cool down, 5 to 10 mins • Stretch	Cross train, 30 mins • Stretch	**INTERVALS** Run, easy pace, 5 mins • Brisk walk, 5 mins. Repeat 2 times • Cool down, 5 to 10 mins • Stretch	Rest day	Bike ride, cross train 45 mins • Stretch	**INTERVALS** Run, easy pace, 5 mins. Brisk walk, 5 mins. Repeat 3 times • Cool down, 5 to 10 mins • Stretch
2	Cross train, 30 mins. Optional: Yoga or Pilates	**INTERVALS** Run, easy pace, 5 mins. Brisk walk, 3 mins. Repeat 3 times • Cool down, 5 to 10 mins • Stretch	Cross train, 30 mins. Optional: Rest day	**INTERVALS** Run, easy pace, 10 mins. Brisk walk, 5 mins. Repeat 2 times • Cool down, 5 to 10 mins • Stretch.	Rest day	**BRISK WALK** Brisk walk, 60 mins • Cool down, 5 to 10 mins • Stretch	**INTERVALS** Run, easy pace, 7 mins. Brisk walk, 3 mins. Repeat 3 times • Cool down, 5 to 10 mins • Stretch
3	Rest Day	**INTERVALS** Warm up, 15 mins • Run, threshold pace, 2 mins. Recovery jog, 2 mins. Repeat 3 times • Cool down, 5 to 10 mins • Stretch	Rest Day	**RECOVERY RUN** Run, easy pace, 25 mins • Cool down, 5 to 10 mins • Stretch	Rest day	Bike ride or cross train, 60 mins • Stretch	**RECOVERY RUN** Run, easy pace, 25 mins • Cool down, 5 to 10 mins • Stretch
4	Cross train, 40 mins • Stretch	**FARTLEK** Run, vary your intensity throughout the workout, 25 mins • Cool down, 5 to 10 mins • Stretch	Rest day	Cross train, 30 mins • Stretch	Rest day	**5K RACE** Run a 5K race.	**RECOVERY RUN** Run, easy pace, 30 mins • Cool down, 5 to 10 mins • Stretch
5	Rest Day	**INTERVALS** Warm up, 15 mins • Run, threshold pace, 3 mins. Recovery jog, 2 mins. Repeat 4 times • Cool down, 5 to 10 mins • Stretch	Cross train, 30 mins • Stretch	Rest day	**FARTLEK** intensity throughout the workout, 25 mins • Cool down, 5 to 10 mins • Stretch	Cross train, 40 mins • Stretch	**LONG RUN** Run, easy pace, 40 mins • Cool down, 5 to 10 mins • Stretch
6	Rest Day	**INTERVALS** Warm up, 15 mins • Run, threshold pace, 3 mins. Recovery jog, 90 secs. Repeat 4 times • Cool down, 5 to 10 mins • Stretch	Cross train, 40 mins • Stretch	**RECOVERY RUN** Run, easy pace, 35 mins • Cool down, 5 to 10 mins • Stretch	Rest day	Swim. Optional: Rest day	**LONG RUN** Run, easy pace, 45 mins • Cool down 5 to 10 mins • Stretch

WEEK 7–12

NOTES

Key days are Day 2, 4 & 7. All other sessions are optional. Do not plan two hard sessions on consecutive days.

Three sessions a week dependent on current fitness levels, then after 3–4 weeks can add a fourth session, after 7–8 weeks can add a fifth

1	2	3	4	5	6	7	WEEK
Rest Day	**INTERVALS** Warm up, 15 mins • Run, threshold pace, 6 mins. Recovery jog, 3 mins. Repeat 2 times • Cool down, 5 to 10 mins • Stretch	Cross train, 40 mins • Stretch	**INTERVALS** Warm up, 8 mins • Run, threshold pace, 60 secs. Recovery jog, 60 secs. Repeat 6 times • Run, easy pace, 10 mins • Cool down, 5 to 10 mins • Stretch	Rest day or Strides	5K Race	**LONG RUN** Run, easy pace, 30 mins • Cool down, 5 to 10 mins • Stretch	7
Rest day or train, 30 minutes. Optional: Yoga or Pilates	**INTERVAL** Warm up, 15 mins • Run, threshold pace, 3 mins. Recovery jog, 90 secs. Repeat 6 times • Cool down, 5 to 10 mins • Stretch	Cross train, 30 mins • Stretch	**THRESHOLD RUN** Run, easy pace, 10 mins • Run, threshold pace, 10 mins • Run, easy pace, 10 mins • Cool down, 5 to 10 mins	Rest day	Bike ride, 60 mins • Stretch	**LONG RUN** Run, easy pace, 60 mins • Cool down, 5 to 10 mins • Stretch	8
Rest Day	**INTERVALS** Warm up, 15 mins • Run, threshold pace, 4 mins. Recovery jog, 90 secs. Repeat 5 times • Cool down, 5 to 10 mins • Stretch	Cross train, 60 mins • Stretch	**THRESHOLD RUN** Warm up, 10 mins • Run, threshold pace, 2 mins. Recovery jog, 1 min. Repeat 6 times • Cool down, 5 to 10 mins • Stretch	Rest day	Cross train, 60 mins • Stretch	**LONG RUN** Run, easy pace, 60 mins • Cool down, 5 to 10 mins • Stretch	9
Rest day	**INTERVALS** Warm up, 15 mins • Run, threshold pace, 10 mins. Recovery jog, 3 mins. Repeat 2 times • Cool down, 5 to 10 mins • Stretch	Rest day	**RECOVERY RUN** Run, easy pace, 30 mins • Cool down, 5 to 10 mins • Stretch	Rest day	Run a 5K race	**LONG RUN** Run, easy pace, 30 mins • Cool down, 5 to 10 mins • Stretch	10
Rest Day	**INTERVALS** Warm up, 15 mins • Run, threshold pace, 3 mins. Recovery jog, 90 secs. Repeat 5 times • Cool down, 5 to 10 mins • Stretch	Rest Day	**THRESHOLD RUN** Run, easy pace, 15 mins • Run, threshold pace, 15 mins • Run, easy pace, 15 mins • Cool down, 5 to 10 mins • Stretch	Rest day	Cross train, 60 mins • Stretch	**LONG RUN** Run, easy pace, 40 mins • Cool down, 5 to 10 mins • Stretch	11
Rest Day	**THRESHOLD RUN** Warm up, 10 mins • Run, threshold pace, 2 mins. Recovery jog, 1 min. Repeat 6 times • Cool down, 5 to 10 mins • Stretch	Rest day	**THRESHOLD RUN** Run, easy pace, 25 mins • Cool down, 5 to 10 mins • Stretch	Rest day	**RECOVERY RUN** Run, easy pace, 10 mins • Cool down, 5 to 10 mins • Stretch	**10k Race**	12

BEGINNERS' HALF-MARATHON PLAN

BY ALAN DENT*

DAY	1	2	3	4	5	6	7
WEEK 1	Walk 40 mins	Rest	Jog 10 mins	Rest	Walk 40 mins	Rest	Jog 10 mins
2	Walk 50 mins	Rest	Jog 15 mins	Rest	Walk 50 mins	Rest	Jog 15 mins
3	Rest	Jog 15 mins	Rest	Run 10 mins	Jog 15 mins	Rest	Run 15 mins
4	Rest	Jog 15 mins	Rest	Jog 15 mins	Rest	Run 15 mins	Rest
5	Jog 15 mins	Rest	Jog 15 mins	Jog 10 mins	Rest	Run 15 mins	Rest
6	Rest	Run 20 mins	Rest	Run 15 mins	Rest	Run 20 mins	Rest
7	Run 30 mins	Rest	**INTERVALS** Jog, 10 mins 3 x 5 mins faster pace with 3 mins jog between 5 mins jog	Rest	Run 20 mins	Rest	Run 20 mins
8	Rest	20 mins, easy run	Rest	**INTERVALS** Jog, 10 mins 8 x 40 secs faster pace with 40 secs jog between 5 mins jog	Rest	30 mins easy	Rest

WEEK 9–16

NOTES

There is a choice of two starting points. For those who are coming to this with very little background of physical activity or feel they want a more gradual introduction, then start at week 1. For those who are more confident or are quite active already, then week 4 would be an appropriate starting point.

* Alan Dent is an experienced runner and Great North Run pace maker. He has a half marathon pb of 67mins 14 sec and marathon pb of 2hr 25 min. He has also represented Great Britain at 5000m and England at cross-country.

DAY

WEEK

1	2	3	4	5	6	7	
30 mins easy jog	Rest	**INTERVALS** 10 mins jog 3 x 5 mins faster pace with 3 mins jog between 5 mins jog	Rest	30 mins easy jog	Rest	Rest	9
40 mins easy	Rest	30 mins easy	Rest	**INTERVALS** 10 min jog 3 x 5 mins faster pace with 3 mins jog between 5 mins jog	Rest	45 mins easy	10
40 mins Aim for a quicker pace than usual	Rest	50 mins easy	Rest	40 mins steady	Rest	55 mins easy	11
Rest	**INTERVALS** 10 mins jog 4 x 5 mins faster pace with 3 mins jog between 5 mins jog	Rest	45 mins run	Rest	Rest	Rest	12
Rest	Rest	70 mins easy	Rest	**INTERVALS** 10 mins jog 4 x 5 mins faster pace with 3 mins jog between 5 mins jog	Rest	80 mins easy	13
30 mins easy	Rest	50 mins easy	Rest	30 mins at a quicker pace	Rest	90 mins easy	14
Rest	Rest	60 mins easy	Rest	30 mins easy	Rest	70 mins easy	15
Rest	Rest	30 min easys	Rest	25 mins easy	Rest	**Half marathon Race**	16

BEGINNERS' MARATHON PLAN

BY ALAN DENT

DAY

WEEK

	1	2	3	4	5	6	7
1	Walk 40 mins	Rest	Jog 10 mins	Rest	Walk 40 mins	Rest	Jog 15 mins
2	Rest	Walk 50 mins	Rest	Jog 20 mins	Rest	Rest	Jog/walk 45 mins
3	Rest	Jog 15 mins	Rest	Jog 20 mins	Rest	Rest	Jog/walk 1 hour
4	Rest	Jog 20 mins	Rest	Run 10 mins	Rest	Jog 15 mins	Longer run 1 hour. Walk for short periods if necessary
5	Rest	Run 30 mins	Rest	Run 30 mins	Rest	Run 30 mins	1 hour – avoid walking if possible
6	Rest	Run 35 mins	Rest	Run 30 mins	Rest	Run 35 mins	1 hour
7	Rest	Run 40 mins	Rest	Run 35 mins	Rest	Run 40 mins	1 hour
8	Rest	Run 40 mins	Run 20 mins	Run 20 mins	Rest	Rest	90 mins or 10k race
9	Rest	Run 30 mins	Run 30 mins	Run 30 mins	Rest	Rest	90 mins
10	Rest	Run 30 mins	Run 45 mins	Run 30 mins	Rest	Rest	90 mins

WEEK 11–20

NOTES

There is a choice of two starting points. For those who are coming to this with very little background of physical activity or feel they want a more gradual introduction, then start at week 1. For those who are more confident or are quite active already then week 4 would be an appropriate starting point.

For a definition of Fartlek, see page 43.

DAY

	1	2	3	4	5	6	7	WEEK
	Rest	Run 30 mins	Run 30 mins	Run 30 mins	Rest	Run 30 mins	Run 90 mins	11
	Rest	Run 30 mins	Run 30 mins	Run 30 mins	Rest	Run 30 mins	Run 2 hours	12
	Rest	Run 30 mins	Rest	Run 50 mins	Rest	Rest	Run 2 hours	13
	Rest	Run 30 mins	Fartlek	Run 30 mins	Rest	Rest	Run 2 hours	14
	Rest	Run 30 mins	1 hour Fartlek	Rest	Rest	Rest	Run 2½ hours	15
	Rest	Run 30 mins	Run 30 mins	Run 30 mins	Rest	Rest	Run 2½ hours or half marathon race	16
	Rest	Run 30 mins	Run 1 hour easy	Run 30 mins	Rest	Rest	Run 3 hours	17
	Rest	Rest	Run 30 mins	1 hour Fartlek	Rest	Run 30 mins	Run 2½ hours	18
	Rest	Run 30 mins	Rest	Run 1 hour easy	Rest	Rest	Run 1 hour	19
	Rest	Run 30 mins	Rest	Run 20 mins easy	Rest	Rest	**Marathon Race**	20

INTERMEDIATE HALF-MARATHON PLAN (SUB-2 HOUR)

BY ALAN DENT

WEEK / DAY

	1	2	3	4	5	6	7
1	Run 5 miles	Rest	Run 3 miles	Run 5 miles	Rest	Run 5 miles	Run 7 miles
2	Rest	Run 5 miles	Rest	Run 5 miles	Rest	Run 5 miles	Run 9 miles
3	Rest	Run 5 miles	Run 7 miles	**INTERVALS** 1 mile warm up • 4 x 5 mins faster pace with 3 mins jog recovery between • 1 mile warm down	Rest	Run 5 miles	Run 10 miles
4	Rest	Run 5 miles	Run 7 miles	Run 8 miles	Rest	Run 6 miles	Run 10 miles
5	Rest	Run 5 miles	Rest	Run 5 miles	Rest	Run 6 miles	10k race or run 12 miles
6	Rest	Run 5 miles	Run 7 miles	**INTERVALS** 1 mile warm up • 8 x 2 mins with 2 mins jog recovery between • 1 mile warm	Rest	Run 6 miles	Run 12 miles

WEEK 7–12

DAY

WEEK

1	2	3	4	5	6	7	
Rest	**INTERVALS** 1 mile warm up • 4 x 5 mins faster pace with 3 mins jog recovery between • 1 mile warm down	Run 5 miles	Warm up • 6 x 3 mins with 3 mins jog recovery	Rest	Run 6 miles	Run 13 miles	7
Rest	**INTERVALS** 1 mile warm up • 5 x 4 min faster pace with 3 mins jog recovery between • 1 mile warm down	Run 5 miles	Run 8 miles at varied pace (fartlek)	Rest	Run 6 miles	Run 15 miles	8
Rest	**INTERVALS** 1 mile warm up • 4 x 5 mins faster pace with 3 mins jog recovery between • 1 mile warm down	Run 5 miles	Run 8 miles	Rest	Run 3 miles easy	10k race or run 15 miles	9
Rest	**INTERVALS**1 mile warm up • 2 x 10 mins with 5 mins jog recovery • 1 mile warm down	Run 5 miles	**INTERVALS** 1 mile warm up • 8 x 3 min with 2 min jog recovery • 1 mile warm down	Rest	Run 6 miles	Run 13 miles	10
Rest	**INTERVALS** 1 mile warm up • 3 x 4 mins with 3 mins jog recovery • Warm down • 1 mile warm down	Run 3 miles	Run 8 miles with some faster bursts/strides	Rest	Run 3 miles	Run 8 miles	11
Rest	Run 6 miles with some faster bursts/strides	Rest	Run 3 miles	Rest	Run 3 miles easy	**Half marathon Race**	12

INTERMEDIATE MARATHON PLAN (SUB-4 HOUR)

BY ALAN DENT

DAY

WEEK

	1	2	3	4	5	6	7
1	Run 5 miles	Rest	Run 5 miles	Rest	Run 5 miles	Rest	Run 8 miles
2	Rest	Run 5 miles	Rest	Run 5 miles	Run 5 miles	Rest	Run 9 miles
3	Rest	Run 6 miles	**INTERVALS** 1 mile warm up • 5 x 1 mins fast with 2 mins jog recovery between • 1 mile warm down	Run 4 miles easy	Rest	Run 6 miles	Run 10 miles
4	Rest	Run 7 miles	**INTERVALS** 1 mile warm up • 2 x 3 mins • 3 mins jog recovery • 1 mile warm down	Run 4 miles	Rest	Run 4 miles easy	Run 11 miles or 10k race
5	Rest	Run 7 miles	**INTERVALS** 1 mile warm up • 2 x 3 mins • 3 mins jog recovery • 1 mile warm down	Run 4 miles	Rest	Run 7 miles easy	Run 12 miles
6	Rest	Run 7 miles	**INTERVALS** 1 mile warm up • 10 x 1 mins • 1 mins jog recovery • 1 mile warm down	Run 6 miles	Rest	Run 6 miles	Run 12 miles
7	Rest	Run 7 miles	**INTERVALS** 1 mile warm up • 3 x 5 mins • 4 mins jog recovery • 1 mile warm down	Run 4 miles	Rest	Run 6 miles	Run 13 miles
8	Rest	Run 2 miles easy • 3 miles tempo pace • 1 mile jog	Run 4 miles easy	**INTERVALS** 1 mile warm up • 10 x 40 seconds uphill, jog back recovery • 1 mile warm down	Rest	Run 6 miles	Run 15 miles

WEEK
9–16

DAY

1	2	3	4	5	6	7	
Rest	Run 6 miles fartlek	Run 4 miles	Run 7 miles easy	Rest	Run 4 miles easy	Half marathon or run 16 miles	9
Rest	Run 6 miles easy	Run 4 miles	Warm up • 4 x 5 min • 3 min jog recovery	Rest	Run 4 miles at proposed marathon pace	Run 13 miles	10
Rest	Run 6 miles fartlek	Run 6 miles	Warm up • 6 mile at marathon pace • Warm down	Rest	Run 4 miles easy	Run 18 miles	11
Rest	**INTERVALS** 1 mile warm up • 6 x 2 mins with 2 mins jog recovery • 1 mile warm down	Run 6 miles	Warm up • 6 mile at marathon pace • Warm down	Rest	Run 4 miles	Run 20 miles	12
Rest	**INTERVALS** 1 mile warm up • 4 x 5 mins • 3 mins jog recovery • 1 mile warm down	Run 6 miles	Run 8 miles fartlek	Rest	Run 4 miles marathon pace	Run 18 miles	13
Rest	**INTERVALS** 1 mile warm up • 8 x 1 mins • 2 mins jog recovery • 1 mile warm down	6 mile	Run 8 miles fartlek	Rest	Run 3 miles marathon pace	Run 20 miles	14
Rest	**INTERVALS** 1 mile warm up • 6 x 2 mins with 2 mins jog recovery • 1 mile warm down	Run 6 miles	Run 5 miles fartlek	Rest	Run 3 miles marathon pace	Run 10 miles easy	15
Rest	**INTERVALS** 1 mile warm up • 8 x 1 min • 2 min jog recovery • 1 mile warm down	Run 4 miles	Rest	Rest	Jog 15 mins	**Marathon Race**	16

ADVANCED HALF-MARATHON PLAN (SUB-1.20)

BY ALAN DENT

DAY

WEEK

	1	2	3	4	5	6	7
1	Run 6 miles	**INTERVALS** 3 x 1 mile at 5k pace • 4 mins jog recovery	Run 5 miles easy	Run 8 miles	Run 6 miles fartlek	Run 4 miles	Run 12 miles
2	Run 4 miles	**INTERVALS** 6 x 3 mins • 2 mins jog recovery	Run 5 miles easy	Run 8 miles	8 x hills at 10k pace • Jog back recovery	Run 4 miles	Run 8 miles
3	Run 6 miles	**INTERVALS** 4 x 1 mile • at 5k pace • 4 mins jog recovery	Run 5 miles easy	Run 8 miles	Run 6 miles fartlok	Run 4 miles	Run 13 miles
4	Run 4 miles	**INTERVALS** 6 x 3 mins • 2 mins jog recovery	Run 5 miles easy	Run 8 miles	Run 6 miles	Run 4 miles	10k race or run 14 miles
5	Run 6 miles	**INTERVALS** 5 x 1 mile or 4 mins • Jog recovery	Run 5 miles easy	Run 8 miles	8 x long hills at 5k pace • Jog back recovery	Run 4 miles	Run 9 miles
6	Run 4 miles	**INTERVALS** 8 x 3 mins • With 2 mins jog recovery	Run 6 miles easy	Run 10 miles	8 x hills at 10k pace • Jog back recovery	Run 5 miles	Run 10 miles
7	Run 6 miles	**INTERVALS** 4 x 1 mile on 3 mins jog recovery	Run 6 miles easy	Run 10 miles	Run 8 miles	Run 4 miles	Run 15 miles
8	Run 4 miles	**INTERVALS** 8 x 3 mins • With 2 mins jog recovery	Run 6 miles easy	Run 8 miles	Run 10 miles fartlek	Run 5 miles	Run 12 miles
9	Run 6 miles	**INTERVALS** 3 x 1 mile on 3 mins jog recovery	Run 6 miles easy	Run 6 miles	Run 6 miles	Run 4 miles	10k race or run 15 miles
10	Run 4 miles	**INTERVALS** 8 x 3 min with 2 mins jog recovery	Run 6 miles easy	Run 10 miles	Run 8 miles fartlek	Run 5 miles	Run 14 miles
11	Run 6 miles	Run 8 miles fartlek	Run 6 mile easys	Run 8 miles	Run 8 miles with strides	Run 4 miles	Run 10 miles
12	Run 4 miles	Run 5 miles with strides	Rest	Run 5 miles	Rest	Run 3 miles with strides	**Half marathon Race**

NOTES

The speed sessions by 1 mile and 3 mins should be preceded by a minimum of 1 mile of warm-up and concluded with 1 mile of warm down.

5k pace or 10k pace refers to the speed at which you would normally run that distance during a race.

Hills should be about 150–200m long.

Long hills should be about 400m long.

For the hill sessions the idea is to run repeated strides at the pre-determined pace and use the jog back down the hill as the recovery. If you find that this type of repetition on a single hill is too tedious you could use a route that incorporates the same number of hills and use the distance between the hills as the recovery.

ADVANCED MARATHON PLAN (SUB-3 HOUR)

BY ALAN DENT

DAY

WEEK

	1	2	3	4	5	6	7
1	Run 6 miles easy	**INTERVALS** 4 x 5 mins at 10k pace • 3 mins jog recovery between	Run 6 miles	**INTERVALS** 2 sets of 8 x 1 mins with 40 seconds recovery • 5 mins between sets	Run 5 miles easy	Run 6 miles	Run 13 miles
2	Run 6 miles easy	**INTERVALS** 8 mile with 8 x short shills • Jog back recovery	Run 6 miles	**INTERVALS** Warm up 6 x 3 mins with 2 mins jog recovery • 6 x 1 min with 1 min jog recovery	Run 5 miles easy	Run 4 miles easy	10k race with 3 miles warm down or 15 miles
3	Run 6 miles easy	**INTERVALS** 4 x 5 mins at 10k pace • 3 mins jog recovery between	Run 6 miles	8 miles fartlek	Run 5 miles easy	Run 5 miles	Run 16 miles
4	Run 6 miles easy	**INTERVALS** 8 x 3 min with 2 mins jog recovery	Run 6 miles	8 mile with 10 x short hill with jog back recovery	Run 5 miles easy	Run 3 miles easy	Half marathon or run 16 miles steady
5	Run 6 miles easy	8 mile fartlek	Run 6 miles	**INTERVALS** 8 mile with 2 x 10 mins with 5 mins recovery	Run 5 miles	Run 5 miles	Run 18 miles
6	Run 6 miles easy	**INTERVALS** 2 (8 x 2 mins) at 5k pace • 1 min jog recovery and 5 mins between sets	Run 4 miles	8 miles with 6 x long hills with jog back recovery	Run 5 miles	Run 5 miles	Run 18 miles
7	Run 6 miles easy	**INTERVALS** 2 x 10 mins at 10k pace • 5 mins jog recovery	Run 6 miles	8 miles tempo run	Run 4 miles easy	Run 6 miles	Run 20 miles
8	Run 6 miles easy	**INTERVALS** 8 x 3 mins at 10k pace • 90 secs jog recovery	Run 6 miles	Run 6 miles	Run 4 miles	Run 4 miles	Half marathon or run 18 miles

WEEK
9–16

DAY / WEEK

1	2	3	4	5	6	7	
Run 6 miles easy	Run 8 miles fartlek	Run 6 miles	INTERVALS 4 x 5 min sat 10k pace • 3 mins jog recovery between	Run 3 miles	Rest	Run 20 miles	9
Run 6 miles easy	INTERVALS 8 miles with 10 x 90 secs with 60 secs jog recovery	Run 7 miles	Run 6 miles start slow and progressively increase pace	Run 6 miles	Run 5 miles	Run 22 miles	10
Run 6 miles easy	6 miles fartlek	Run 7 miles	Run 3 miles at marathon pace • 1 mile jog • 3 miles at 10 secs faster than marathon pace	Run 4 miles	Rest	Run 22 miles	11
Run 6 miles easy	INTERVALS 8 x 3 mins with 2 mins jog recovery	Run 6 miles	Run 8 miles at marathon pace	Run 4 miles	Run 4 miles	10k race or run 15 miles	12
Run 6 miles easy	6 miles fartlek	Run 6 miles	4-miles tempo run	Run 4 miles	Run 3 miles	Run 20 miles	13
Run 6 miles easy	INTERVALS 8 x 3 mins at 10k pace • 90 secs jog recovery	Run 4 miles	Run 8 miles at marathon pace	Run 4 miles	Rest	Run 20 miles	14
Run 6 miles easy	INTERVALS 6 mile with 8 x 1 mins • 2 mins jog recovery	Run 6 miles	Jog 1 mile • 5 miles brisk • Jog 1 mile at tempo	Rest	Run 6 miles	Run 10 miles	15
Run 6 miles easy	Run 5 miles with some easy strides	Rest	Run 4 miles	Rest	Run 3 miles with some easy strides	**Marathon Race**	16

NOTES

The speed sessions should be preceded by a minimum of 1 mile of warm up and concluded with 1 mile of warm down.

5k pace or 10k pace refers to the speed at which you would normally run that distance during a race.

Short hills should be about 150–200m long.

Long hills should be about 400m long.

For the hill sessions the idea is to run repeated strides at the pre-determined pace and use the jog back down the hill as the recovery. If you find that this type of repetition on a single hill is too tedious you could use a route that incorporates the same number of hills and use the distance between the hills as the recovery.

ADVANCED MARATHON PLAN (SUB-2.45)

BY RICHARD NERURKAR*

DAY

WEEK	1	2	3	4	5	6	7	TOTAL
1	**a.m.** 5 miles easy **p.m.** 5 miles steady	6 × 3 mins, 2 mins	**a.m.** 5 miles easy **p.m.** 5 miles steady	5 miles fartlek	4 miles easy or rest	5 miles steady	14 miles	50
2	**a.m.** 5 miles easy **p.m.** 5 miles steady	8 × 150m hills	**a.m.** 5 miles easy **p.m.** 5 miles steady	5-mile tempo run	5 miles easy	5 miles steady	16 miles	55
3	**a.m.** 5 miles easy **p.m.** 5 miles steady	4 × 1 mile, 2 mins	**a.m.** 5 miles easy **p.m.** 5 miles steady	6 × 250m hills	5 miles easy	2 miles easy + strides	10k/10-mile race	50
4	**a.m.** 5 miles easy **p.m.** 5 miles steady	10 × 2 mins, 2 mins	**a.m.** 5 miles easy **p.m.** 5 miles steady	3 × 2k, 3 mins	**a.m.** 5 miles easy **p.m.** 5 miles steady	5 miles steady	18 miles	60
5	**a.m.** 5 miles easy **p.m.** 5 miles steady	8 × 150m hills	**a.m.** 5 miles easy **p.m.** 5 miles steady	6 miles easy + strides	Rest	2–3 miles easy	10–20-mile race	50–60
6	5 miles easy	6 miles fartlek	**a.m.** 5 miles easy **p.m.** 5 miles steady	8 × 1k, 3 mins	**a.m.** 5 miles easy **p.m.** 5 miles steady	Timed run over 8 miles	20 miles	65
7	**a.m.** 5 miles easy **p.m.** 5 miles steady	1-2-3-4-3-2-1 min pyramid	**a.m.** 5 miles easy **p.m.** 5 miles steady	4 × 2k, 3 mins	**a.m.** 5 miles easy **p.m.** 5 miles steady	5 miles steady	22 miles	70+
8	**a.m.** 5 miles easy **p.m.** 5 miles steady	2 × 1 mile, 2 mins + 2 × ½ mile, 90secs + 4 × 400m, 1 min	5 miles easy	5 miles easy + strides	Rest	2–3 miles easy	Half marathon race	45
9	5 miles easy	6 miles steady or easy fartlek	**a.m.** 5 miles easy **p.m.** 5 miles steady	3 × 3k, 3 mins	**a.m.** 5 miles easy **p.m.** 5 miles steady	8 × 2 mins, 2 min	24 miles	75
10	5 miles easy	**a.m.** 4 miles easy **p.m.** 7 miles brisk	5 miles easy + strides	2 × 5km*, 4 min	5 miles easy	6 miles steady	15 miles	55
11	6 miles easy	6 miles fartlek	5 miles easy	8 miles brisk	Rest	5 miles steady + strides	10 miles	40
12	5 miles easy	2 × 1 mile*, 2 min	Rest	3 miles easy + strides	Rest	2 miles easy or rest	**Marathon Race**	15 + race

* Richard Nerurkar had a number of top-five finishes at the World and European Championships

Thanks to following this plan I achieved my marathon PB.

Right: Running legend Richard Nerurkar

ADVANCED MARATHON PLAN (SUB-2.20)

BY RICHARD NERURKAR

DAY

WEEK	1	2	3	4	5	6	7	TOTAL
1	**a.m.** 6 miles easy **p.m.** 6 miles steady	**a.m.** 4 miles easy **p.m.** 4 × 1 mile, 2 mins	12 miles easy	**a.m.** 6 miles easy **p.m.** 8 miles steady	6 miles easy	8 miles inc. 20 mins fartlek	16 miles	80
2	**a.m.** 6 miles easy **p.m.** 6 miles steady	**a.m.** 4 miles easy **p.m.** 3 × 3k, 3 mins	12 miles easy	**a.m.** 6 miles easy **p.m.** 8 miles steady + strides	**a.m.** 4 miles easy **p.m.** 6 × 800m, 2 mins	Rest	18 miles	80
3	**a.m.** 6 miles easy **p.m.** 6 miles steady	**a.m.** 5 miles easy **p.m.** 8 × 1k, 90secs	13 miles easy	**a.m.** 5 miles easy **p.m.** 6–7 miles fartlek	8 miles steady	40-min tempo run	18–20 miles	90
4	**a.m.** 6 miles easy **p.m.** 6 miles steady	**a.m.** 5 miles easy **p.m.** 4 × (1600m + 400m), 1 min/2 mins	13 miles easy	**a.m.** 5 miles easy **p.m.** 5 miles easy + strides	Rest	4 miles easy	10k race	65
5	**a.m.** 6 miles easy **p.m.** 6 miles steady	16 miles easy	**a.m.** 6 miles easy **p.m.** 10 miles steady	**a.m.** 5 miles easy **p.m.** 4 × 2k at marathon pace, 1k at 30 secs slower	Rest	**a.m.** 8 miles inc. 20 × 30s, 30secs **p.m.** 4 miles easy	20 miles	90
6	**a.m.** 6 miles easy **p.m.** 10 miles steady	**a.m.** 6 miles easy **p.m.** 6 × 1 mile, 2 min	14 miles easy	**a.m.** 5 miles easy **p.m.** 8 miles easy + strides	**a.m.** 5 miles easy **p.m.** 5 miles steady	4 miles easy	**Half marathon Race**	90

WEEK 7–12

I tried to stick to this schedule in the build-up to my 2012 London Marathon but ran it all at my own pace, rather than at the pace of a runner aiming for sub 2.20.

1	2	3	4	5	6	7	TOTAL	WEEK
Rest	5 miles easy	8 miles easy	**a.m.** 5 miles easy **p.m.** 5 miles easy	10 miles steady	8 miles inc. 20 mins fartlek	22–24 miles	70	7
a.m. 6 miles easy **p.m.** 6 miles steady	5 × 2k at marathon pace, 1k 30 secs slower	14 miles easy	**a.m.** 6 miles easy **p.m.** 6 miles steady	**a.m.** 5 miles easy **p.m.** 10 × 2 mins, 90 secs	10 miles easy	24 miles	95	8
a.m. 6 miles easy **p.m.** 6 miles steady	**a.m.** 6 miles easy **p.m.** 2 × 2 miles, 2 mins + 2 × 1 mile, 90 secs	14 miles easy	**a.m.** 6 miles easy **p.m.** 10 miles steady	**a.m.** 5 miles easy **p.m.** 5 miles steady	8 miles inc. 20 × 30 secs, 30 secs	20-mile tempo run	100	9
Rest	**a.m.** 5 miles easy **p.m.** 6 miles steady	10 miles easy	10 miles easy	**a.m.** 5 miles easy **p.m.** 6 miles steady	**a.m.** 2 × (8 × 400m, 45 secs), 3 mins **p.m.** 5 miles easy	14 miles	75	10
Rest	**a.m.** 4 miles easy **p.m.** 2 × 6k at marathon pace, 4 mins	**a.m.** 5 miles easy **p.m.** 5 miles steady	6 miles easy	**a.m.** 7 miles inc. 20 × 30 secs, 30 secs; **p.m.** 5 miles easy	Rest	12 miles	55	11
5 miles easy	8–10 miles steady finishing briskly	Rest	4 miles easy + strides	Rest	2–3 miles easy	**Race**	20 + race	12

REFERENCES

CHAPTER 1: GETTING GOING

1. NHS. 'Benefits Of Exercise' <http://www.nhs.uk/Livewell/fitness/Pages/whybeactive.aspx> [Accessed 2013]

2. NHS. 'Physical Activity Guidelines For Adults' <http://www.nhs.uk/Livewell/fitness/Pages/physical-activity-guidelines-for-adults.aspx> [Accessed 2013]

3. Fries, James.F. Chakravarty, E.F. Hubert, H.B. Lingala, V.B. (2008 Stanford University School of Medicine), 'Reduced disability and mortality among aging runners: a 21-year longitudinal study' <http://www.ncbi.nlm.nih.gov/pubmed/18695077> [Accessed 2013]

4. Christie Aschwanden. 'Runners are not giving themselves arthritis', The Washington Post, 12 August 2013 <http://articles.washingtonpost.com/2013-08-12/national/41318400_1_osteoarthritis-hip-replacement-joints>[Accessed 2013] which cites study by Williams, P.T. (2013) 'Effects of running and walking on osteoarthritis and hip replacement risk' <http://www.ncbi.nlm.nih.gov/pubmed/23377837 > [Accessed 2013]

5. Duffield, R. Cannon, J. King, M. (2010), 'The effects of compression garments on recovery of muscle performance following high-intensity sprint and plyometric exercise' <http://www.ncbi.nlm.nih.gov/pubmed/19131276> [Accessed 2014]

6. Ridge, Sarah. T. Johnson, Wayne. A. Mitchell, Ulrike. H. Hunter, Iain. Robinson, Eric. Brent, Rich. S.E. Brown, Stephen Douglas. (2013 Brigham Young University) 'Foot Bone Marrow Edema After a 10-wk Transition to Minimalist Running Shoes' < http://www.medscape.com/viewarticle/807314> [Accessed 2013]

7. American College of Sports Medicine guidelines on stretching http://www.acsm.org [Accessed 2014]

CHAPTER 3: PREVENTING AND DEALING WITH INJURY

1. O'Mara, Kelly. 'How Long Does It Take To Get Out Of Shape?' Competitor, 27 March 2014, <http://running.competitor.com/2013/05/training/how-long-does-it-take-to-get-out-of-shape_70267 > [Accessed 2014)

2. Ready, E. A. Quinney, H. A. 'Alterations in anaerobic threshold as the result of endurance training and detraining' (1982) <http://runnersconnect.net/running-training-articles/how-long-does-it-take-to-lose-your-running-fitness/ [Accessed 2014]

3. Spencer, Ben. 'Exercise can help even in your 90s: Tests find elderly who did vigorous fitness work had improved strength and balance', Daily Mail, 20 January 2014, < http://www.dailymail.co.uk/health/article-2542395/Even-90s-exercise-help-Tests-elderly-did-vigorous-fitness-work-improved-strength-balance.html > [Accessed 2014]

CHAPTER 4: FOOD FOR FUEL

1. No author listed. 'Running suppresses cravings for unhealthy foods such as pizzas and burgers, new research reveals', Daily Record, 30 January, 2014 < http://www.dailyrecord.co.uk/news/scottish-news/running-suppresses-cravings-unhealthy-foods-3093550 > [Accessed 2014]

2. Res, P.T. Groen, B. Pennings, B. Beelen, M. Wallis, G.A. Gijsen, A.P. Senden, J.M, Van Loon, L.J. (2012) 'Protein ingestion before sleep improves postexercise overnight recovery' <http://www.ncbi.nlm.nih.gov/pubmed/22330017> [Accessed 2014]

3. Murphy, M. Eliot, K, Heuertz, R.M. Weiss, E. (2012), 'Whole beetroot consumption acutely improves running performance' <http://www.ncbi.nlm.nih.gov/

pubmed/22709704>[Accessed 2014]

4. Pritchett, K, Pritchett. R. 'Chocolate Milk: a post-exercise recovery beverage for endurance sports' (2012) www.ncbi.nim.gov/pubmed/23075563 (Accessed 2014)

CHAPTER 5: JUST FOR WOMEN

1. RCOG statement 4 (2004), 'Exercise in pregnancy' <http://www.rcog.org.uk/womens-health/clinical-guidance/exercise-pregnancy> [Accessed 2014]

2. NHS (2013), 'Exercise in pregnancy' < http://www.nhs.uk/conditions/pregnancy-and-baby/pages/pregnancy-exercise.aspx?tabname=Pregnancy#close> [Accessed 2014]

3. Macrae, Fiona. 'Exercise when you're pregnant and you'll have a brighter baby', *Daily Mail*, 11 November, 2013 http://www.dailymail.co.uk/sciencetech/article-2498974/Exercise-youre-pregnant-youll-brighter-baby.html [Accessed 2014]

4. Cary, G.B. Quinn, T.J. (2001) 'Exercise and lactation: are they compatible?' <http://www.ncbi.nlm.nih.gov/pubmed/11173670> [Accessed 2014]

5. Gregory, A. L. Davies, Larry. A. Wolfe, Mottola, Michelle. F. MacKinnon, Catherine (2003), 'Exercise in Pregnancy and the Postpartum Period' <http://www.nrcresearchpress.com/doi/abs/10.1139/h03-024#.Uxitcc6dtNo> [Accessed 2014]

6. Warner, Jennifer, 'Study Shows Regular Exercise Improves Mental and Physical Health of Menopausal Women', WebMD, 24 March, 2006 <http://www.webmd.com/menopause/news/20060324/exercise-eases-menopause-symptoms> [Accessed 2014] citing study by Villaverde Gutiérrez, Carman. Torres Luque, Gema. Ábalos Medina, Grazia. M. Argente del Castillo, Maria. J. Guisado, Isabel. M. Guisado Barrilao, Rafael and Ramírez Rodrigo, Jesus (2012), 'Influence of exercise on mood in postmenopausal women' http://onlinelibrary.wiley.com/doi/10.1111/j.1365-2702.2011.03972.x/abstract [Accessed 2014]

CHAPTER 6: THE ULTIMATE CHALLENGE – RUNNING A MARATHON

1. Schwartz, Robert.S. Merkel Kraus, Stacia. Schwartz, Jonathan.G. Wickstrom, Kelly.K. Peichel, Gretchen. Garberich, Ross. F. Lesser, John. R. Oesterle, Stephen.N. Knickelbine, Thomas. Harris, Kevin.M. Duval, Sue. Roberts, William O. O'Keefe, James.H. (2014), 'Increased Coronary Artery Plaque Volume Among Male Marathon Runners' <http://www.msma.org/docs/communications/MoMed/Hearts_Breaking_Over_Marathon_Running_MarApr2014_Missouri_Medicine.pdf> [Accessed 2014]

USEFUL WEBSITES

womensrunninguk.co.uk • mensrunninguk.co.uk • marathontalk.com • runnersworld.co.uk

parkrun.org.uk • virginmoneylondonmarathon.com • athleticsweekly.com • runningfitnessmag.co.uk

britishathletics.org.uk • runengland.org • runbritain.com • therunningbug.co.uk

theguardian.com/lifeandstyle/the-running-blog

RECOMMENDED BOOKS

Bean, Anita, *Food For Fitness*, 4th ed, Bloomsbury, 2014

Kowalchik, Claire, *The Complete Book Of Running For Women*, Simon & Schuster, 1999

McDougall, Christopher, *Born To Run*, Profile Books, 2010

Nerurkar, Richard, *Marathon Running*, A & C Black, 2008

Noakes, Tim, *Lore Of Running*, Human Kinetics Europe Ltd, 2002

Radcliffe, Paula, *Paula: My Story So Far*, Pocket Books, 2005

Yelling, Liz, *The Woman's Guide to Running*, Hamlyn, 2006

LAST WORD AND THANKS

Firstly, I would like to thank Lucy as without her shared passion for running and honest, down-to-earth approach, this book would never had happened.

One of the special things about this guide is that it contains real people of all abilities talking about their running experiences – both good and bad – which we can all relate to and learn from. So thank you for taking the time to share your inspirational stories Nicola Kukuc, Abi Wright, Andrea Chapman, Jack Brooks, Tish Jones, Jamie Singer, Liz Yelling, Christina Smith, Rosie Millard, June Allen, Sarah Kinsella, Vicky Doherty, Dean Piper, Amy Whitehead and Hazel Ponsford.

Findlay Young, thank you for sharing how running – as well as your own strength and determination – got you through some very tough times following your cancer diagnosis. You have helped so many other people along the way and I am honoured to say I have met you – I still remember waiting at the end of the Great North Run to give you a big kiss when you had a huge bandage on your head.

Also, many thanks to my mum, Nancy, who not only shared her story but has put up with me constantly pestering her to go running! I am glad you have achieved far more than you ever thought you would. Considering you say you never liked running at school, you haven't done badly. You have always given me invaluable advice on parenting and work (from this book to other job opportunities) and on making perfect Yorkshire puds – thank you.

Big thank yous must also go to the experts who have generously given their time and lent their expertise to enhance this book. I'm grateful to you all – Dr Juliet McGrattan for your input on all things medical; physiotherapist Mark Buckingham (wpbphysio.co.uk) for your advice on injury prevention, rehabilitation and exercising when pregnant and his colleague Jean Johnson for her expertise on women's health; physio Sam Bishop (PACETherapies.co.uk) for sharing his tips on injury prevention and Lucy's mum Sandy Waterlow for explaining the importance of sports massage; running experts Liz Yelling (yellingperformance.com), Richard Nerurkar and Sensev El-Ahmadi (hwrc.me.uk) for their training advice and schedules; dietician Nichola Whitehead (nicsnutrition.com) for her tips on healthy eating and Julia Buckley (juliabuckley.co.uk) for her advice on running to lose weight. Thanks also to Alan Dent (dentysrunningblog.blogspot.com) for providing the training schedules – your many years of running experience are invaluable to us all.

I'd also like to thank Eddie MacDonald for taking many of the great pictures you can see in this book – you really are the king of running pictures!

Finally I'd like to thank my followers on Twitter for adding their personal touch by providing their tips.

So whatever your reason to run... keep on running!

INDEX

PICTURE CREDITS